THE
Archive Photographs
SERIES

CARDIFF
remembered

THE
Archive Photographs
SERIES
CARDIFF
remembered

by
Brian Lee

CHALFORD

First published 1997
Copyright © Brian Lee, 1997

The Chalford Publishing Company
St Mary's Mill, Chalford,
Stroud, Gloucestershire, GL6 8NX

ISBN 0 7524 0718 X

Typesetting and origination by
The Chalford Publishing Company
Printed in Great Britain by
Bailey Print, Dursley, Gloucestershire

This book is dedicated to the memory of my mother who, known as 'Girlie' Donovan, was born and bred in the Frederick Street area of Cardiff.

CONTENTS

Brian Lee and Frank Hennessy at Maindy Stadium, 1996.

I have also enjoyed broadcasting with Brian on BBC Radio Wales on several occasions. Even though the first time I interviewed him, outside The Anthonys public house in Ely, a stray, barking dog did its utmost to spoil the proceedings!

In *Cardiff Remembered*, Brian captures the essence of so many aspects of Cardiff's colourful past and takes us on a fascinating journey into our rich heritage, evoking many historical events and much-loved characters.

The reader will find in the ensuing pages humour, sacrifice, glory and tragedy, indeed, many of the ingredients that have combined to make Cardiff what it is today. To give readers a further taste of what is to come let me ask these questions. When did Buffalo Bill visit Cardiff? How did the legendary Billy the Seal come to be a resident of Victoria Park? Which famous pirate once lived at Llanrumney Hall? Where was the Continental Waxworks?

Read on, and all will be revealed in this unique book which will give many hours of pleasure to Cardiffians and visitors alike. I am certain that you will enjoy reading *Cardiff Remembered*. I know I did.

Frank Hennessy

FOREWORD

I was delighted when Brian Lee asked me to write the foreword to this admirable book. For I have had the pleasure of reading his popular 'Looking Back' series of articles on old Cardiff in the *Cardiff Independent* and more recently his 'Bygone Cardiff' column in the *South Wales Echo*.

INTRODUCTION

Cardiff Remembered is somewhat different to its predecessors in the splendid Archive Photographs series in that it does not deal with one or two districts of a particular town or city. It is true that a lot of the action, so to speak, takes place in the central area of Cardiff and the building of the City Hall, the old Town Hall, the Animal Wall, the old Central Library are featured. However, there is more than the occasional excursion outside the central area of Cardiff and 'visits' are paid to Roath Park and Victoria Park, Maindy Stadium, the Docks area, Llanrumney, as well as many other places besides.

The other difference is that *Cardiff Remembered*, as the title of the book suggests, contains the reminiscences or recollections of a number of Cardiffians, some of whom have been a long time gone. For example, one Cardiffian recalls the time barges loaded with grain and flour travelled along the old Glamorganshire Canal to be stored in the canal company's warehouse.

Cardiff's most famous animal – Billy the Seal – is naturally remembered by a number of people and in this year, 1997, which sees the centenary of the opening of Victoria Park, a statue of a seal will be unveiled in Billy's memory. To think that at one time, during the First World War when the cost of feeding Billy was questioned, there was a proposal put forward that 'he' be destroyed!

There are still some Cardiffians who can remember Ely Racecourse. It is certainly fondly recalled by many former trainers and jockeys. The Welsh Grand National was held there between 1895 and 1939 and included in this book are some excellent photographs of the 1926 winner Miss Balscadden, ridden by local man, David Thomas.

Another piece of Cardiff entertainment recalled is the Continental Waxworks that used to be in St Mary Street. It closed in 1946 but some Cardiffians will remember seeing some of the exhibits at Coney Beach showground near Porthcawl in the 1950s. The photographs of the old Guildford Crescent Swimming Baths, meanwhile, will bring back, I am sure, many memories to some of the hundreds of Cardiffians who, like myself, learned to swim there.

For some of the earlier memories and recollections I have relied on John Kyrle Fletcher's *Cardiff Notes: Picturesque and Biographical* (1920) and W.J. Trounce's *Cardiff in the Fifties* (1918). Another valuable source of information has been the six volumes of records of the County Borough of Cardiff, edited by John Hobson Matthews, and published by the Corporation in 1898.

Finally, a word or two on how this book came to be written. A few years ago, I used to write a weekly 'Looking Back' column for the now sadly defunct *Cardiff Independent* free newspaper. The nicest part of the job was receiving letters and photographs from my readers. Some of those readers suggested that I should write a book including some of the articles I had written as they had brought back happy memories of a Cardiff much different to the one we know today. Last year I wrote to Margaret O'Reilly, education correspondent of the *South Wales Echo*, telling her of my plans to publish a book on old Cardiff. She very kindly gave my proposed book a plug in the paper. Luckily for me the article was read by Simon Eckley, Project Editor at Chalford Publishing, who lives in Cardiff. The rest, as they say and most appropriately in this case, is history.

Brian J. Lee
April 1997

CHAPTER 1

Streets, buildings and public houses

Spital Cottages, Crockherbtown, 1883.

Queen Street, c. 1910, when horse and carts were in abundance.

Crockherbtown and Queen Street

The name Crockherbtown (1776), also Crockarton (1348) and Crockerstrete (1399), is thought to have originated from the fact that pot herbs, or crock herbs, were cultivated in the area by the monks of Greyfriars.

William Rees, author of *Cardiff: A History of the City*, writes: '*In 1855, Queen Street within the walls was said scarcely to deserve the name of a street for it was merely a lane with about twenty-four houses linking St John Street to Crockerton, the presence of the weighing machine obstructing the street and its approach*'.

The Cardiff to London stagecoach used to pass through Crockherbtown and the first letter box in Cardiff was erected there in 1855. In 1886 when the Town Council changed the name

'Crockherbtown' to Queen Street there were many objections. Alas, all to no avail. A *Cardiff Directory* for 1858 informs us that on the approach to the villas in Crockherbtown there were to be found neatly-kept flower beds while dwarf shrubs and evergreens gave graceful taste to the increasing number of respectable inhabitants.

One of these inhabitants had this to say about his house: '*It has a beautiful old fashioned and wonderfully productive garden. I grew figs and mulberries there, and there was mistletoe growing on the apple trees. In those days the theatre stood about where the Park Hotel stands now, and there was a lane known as Bradley's Lane going up where Park Place is. Mr Bradley's father was a hunting man and had a large stables in Womanby Street.*'

Sam Allen in his *Reminiscences*, published in 1918, tells us that: '*One of my* early recollections is a visit to the old Theatre Royal [in Crockherbtown]. It was during a Christmas pantomime in the early 1860s. Cinderella was being produced, with a ballet of about six fat ladies in abbreviated costumes... Years after, the historical old theatre was burnt to the ground when the Philharmonic was being erected.'

1884. 'The effect of his epigrammatic lecture was somewhat marred by the Philistine demonstration of some of the well-known 'dock boys', who promenaded the rear of the hall displaying gigantic sun flowers, tiger lilies, and suchlike, somewhat to that aesthetic gentleman's discomfiture.'

Oscar Wilde v the Dock Boys

Sam Allen also recalls the time when the celebrated Oscar Wilde visited the Queen Street Hall Exhibition in

The Lady Blacksmith of Paradise Place

The *Cardiff Records* tell us that Paradise Place was: '*A narrow street off the south side of Crockherbtown, paral-*

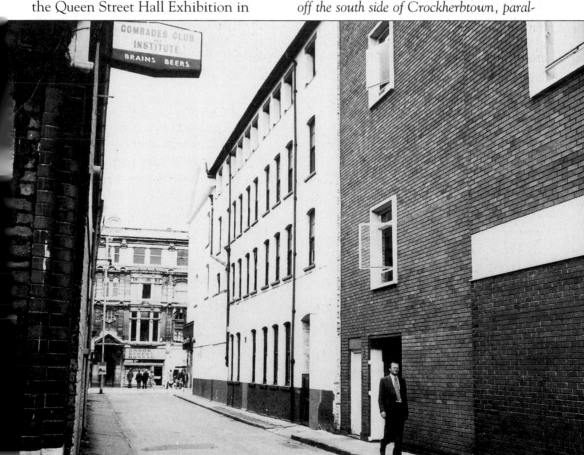

Paradise Place – once the site of picturesque cottages – c. 1950.

11

lel with the west side of Charles Street'. However, Sam Allen gives us a much better description of the Paradise Place of the 1860s: *'The name Paradise Place sounds highly poetical, and no-one today would associate that locality with the Garden of Eden, yet some of us can remember very picturesque little suburban cottages, with pretty front gardens, and quite a natty little blacksmith's shop. Here, through an open window was to be seen a lady blacksmith, wielding a clumsy short-handled hammer, and pounding away on a short length of white-hot nail rod, about a quarter of an inch square. These rods were rolled especially for nail making, probably at the College Works near the Cow and Snuffers at Llandaff. A little bellows, perched overhead, and operated by a sort of* bell rope, supplied the necessary blast, and another, considerably smaller, such as was in common use for kitchen purposes, sent a small jet of air, which blew away the scale from the nail in course of making. A fixed cutter in the anvil was the principal appliance required for making the larger number of strong nails used, by past generations, for horse shoeing, and other purposes.'

Frederick Street

On 14 December 1846, the town council ordered that the fairs and cattle markets in Frederick Street, where the Cardiff County Council library now stands, be moved to St Mary

Frederick Street, c. 1950.

Kingsway. The Red Lion Hotel is to the right of picture.

Street. The *Cardiff Street Directory* for 1855 informs us that some of the residents of Frederick Street then were John Dodds, a cowkeeper and milkman; William Hume, Deputy governor of Cardiff Prison; Rowland Harris, a veterinary surgeon; and John Palmer, an undertaker. In those days, Frederick Street was little more than a country road and the big houses that were built there were much-sought-after residences. Later on these houses made way for other premises and little cottage-type houses. The Queen Street end of Frederick Street had a number of warehouses, the first of any size being built in 1908 for the Leicester Hosiery Company. It was in Frederick Street in January 1917 that Cardiff saw its greatest-ever fire when the five-floor Glamorgan Insurance Building was burnt to the ground.

Frederick Street also had its share of public houses. There was the Burnham Inn (1897), Bute Castle Hotel (1863), Castle Brewery (1855), Manchester Unity Tavern (1858), Marchioness of Bute Inn (1855), King's Head Tavern (1858), Stag and Hounds (1897), Ivorites Arms (1855) and Pembroke Castle Inn. The pubs in Little Frederick Street were the Shamrock and Leek Tavern (1858), Joiners Arms (1858), Dublin Arms (1897) and one that some Cardiffians will have memories of – The Lifeboat (1897).

For a short while during the Second World War, I lived in Frederick Street with my maternal grandparents as my mother was in hospital. During the air-raids we would dash across the road from No 59 Frederick Street to Canada House where we would take shelter, sur-

Kingsway, c. 1950. The Rose & Crown has been renamed Coopers.

rounded by hanging sides of bacon, from Hitler's Luftwaffe. It was outside Canada House that my sister, Valerie, broke my collar bone by swinging me around and letting me go. Other memories include seeing the Hancocks Brewery horses pulling the beer wagon through the street. Then there was my Nana Donovan's black cat that was so fierce that no dog would dare to go near it and Grandpa Donovan putting cheese and onions on a tin plate over the open coal fire. Young men played pitch and toss and my uncles Philip, Billy and Jackie knocked down stacked tin cans on the banks of the nearby Glamorgan Canal.

The Pound and the Town Wall

Many Cardiffians will remember the ladies and gentlemen's toilets that used to be in Kingsway. But how many of those who can recall them realize that where the gentlemen's lavatory stood was once the site of the town pound?

The Pound, as it was known, had a hole in one of the walls where farmers could see if any of their strayed horses or cows had been impounded. The same spot, many years earlier of course, had been the site of the North Gate of the town wall and all traffic to or from the north had to pass under a castellated tower.

Kingsway, c. 1950. The gentlemen's toilet was built on the site of the town pound.

The town wall, which was some ten feet high and six to eight feet thick, had been constructed in the 14th century and the longest surviving section of it near The Hayes finally vanished in 1901 when it was pulled down to make way for the old Fish Market, a site to be later occupied by the South Wales Electricity Board's showroom.

Mass at The Red Lion

The Red Lion Hotel, which used to stand on the corner of Kingsway and Queen Street, was built in 1792. During the early part of the 19th centu- ry the town's Catholics would gather there in the 'ordinary room' of the inn to hear Mass as there was no Roman Catholic church in the area at the time. The officiating priest travelled from town to town in South Wales, probably on horseback. The Red Lion was still standing as late as 1958 and in the 1930s it is known that a Mrs E. Potter was the landlady.

Duke Street, c. 1920. This was known as Shoemaker Street between 1536 and 1810.

Duke Street and Robert of Normandy

Does Duke Street owe its name to the sojourn of the Duke of Normandy in Cardiff Castle for more than 25 years? Or does the name originate from 'Duckstreete' as it was known in 1563? It would be nice to think, perhaps, that the former explanation was true. The son of William the Conqueror, Robert, Duke of Normandy, was said to have a better claim to the throne than his younger brother, Henry I who defeated and captured him at the battle of Tenchebrai.

According to the *Morganiae Archaeiographia* (1578): '*between the gates of faire broad way leading up to the Keep was a very deepe darke dungeon wherein Robert Curthose, Duke of Normandy, was detayned and dyed*'.

Apparently the poor Duke, who was eighty when he died, spent the last 26 years of his life in solitary confinement in Cardiff Castle. To make it more difficult for him to escape – he tried on at least one occasion – his brother gave orders that his eyes were to be 'put out'. Some ancient scribes maintain that during his long captivity he was treated 'with great rigour and severity'. Others contended that 'with great kindness and leniency' he was afforded every luxury and amusement. Local legend that he was imprisoned in the Blaketower (Black Tower), however, is simply not true. It wasn't even built at the time of his incarceration!

16

Cardiff in 1829

A visitor to the little town of Cardiff 150 years ago would have found the debtor's prison, town hall, and butter market all situated in High Street and handily placed near the old quay. The fact that High Street was considered to be the best business street in Cardiff so annoyed the tradesmen of Duke Street that in 1829 they issued a broadsheet proclaiming their wares. The landlords of the Olde Green Dragon, New Dragon, Crown and Anchor, The Three Tuns and The Glove and Shears, prepared a joint advertisement claiming that the wines and beers at their hostelries were 'The finest in Cardiff and superior to those inns in High Street'. The landlord of The Three Tuns also boasted that for the convenience of his patrons a passage led from The Three Tuns to the High Street meat market.

Among the tradesmen a visitor would have found in Duke Street in 1829 were: W. Allen, baker and confectioner, and E. Young the mercers and drapers. Mr D. Evans, meanwhile, claimed to sell 'the safest drugs in town' while the 'best' china tea could be obtained from Smith and French the grocers. Other shopkeepers who advertised their wares were C.C. Williams, currier and leather merchant, J. Wheeler, architect and W. Reed who was a bookbinder, printer and bookseller.

Before the advent of the railway, the London to Milford coach used to pass through Duke Street, which in those days was only 14 ft wide in places. The sewer system consisted of open gullies and a nearby brook was often polluted by tannery refuse.

High Street, 1865. The Three Horse Shoes can be seen to the left of the picture.

St Mary Street, 1891.

Bute

Visitors to Cardiff more than a hundred years ago would have seen, as the picture on page 17 shows, the statue to Lord Bute in High Street and not, where it now stands, in the centre of the roundabout in St Mary Street. Kyrle Fletcher (*Cardiff Notes: Picturesque & Biographical*) writes: '*This Lord Bute has a full right to stand here and look up the street at his Castle entrance, for he was the maker of modern Cardiff. He saw its possibilities even in those early days, when the coal came down the canal barges to a tiny basin at the mouth of the Taff, and he poured his wealth into the scheme for building docks to meet the future trade which was to make Cardiff the chief coaling port of the world, and the port with the largest export trade.*'

The Russian Cannon

Visitors would also have seen a Russian cannon which can also be identified, albeit not very clearly, in the picture on page 17. This cannon was presented to Cardiff Corporation by the War Office in recognition of the townsmen's contribution in the struggle to capture the Great Redoubt at the Battle of Alma under heavy enemy fire. Several soldiers from Cardiff are said to have lost their lives, and Corporal Shields, who was awarded the Victoria Cross, was a native of the town.

Old St Mary Street

Kyrle Fletcher gives us a fascinating glimpse into the history of our city. Writing about the St Mary Street of yesteryear he has this to say: 'Once upon a time St Mary Street was made up of town houses of the local gentry, Lewis of the Van, Mathews of Llandaff, Bassett of Beau Pr'e, each had their office and town residence to which they could come in the winter months. In the reign of Queen Elizabeth these local gentry were constantly fighting in a royal manner. Then the bellman (town crier) of Cardiff would ring his bell and order all the Queen's loyal subjects to go into their homes. This was usually the signal for much window breaking, a stab or two with a dagger and then the sequel, a long drawn-out case in the Star Chamber.

But of those houses not a trace remains – the builder has always been a busy man in Cardiff. The old Town Hall has gone; its heavy gloomy corridors and pillared doorway will no more echo to the tread of the Sheriff's stout javelin men.'

Murder near the Philharmonic

A stabbing in St Mary Street many years later in the 1920s had much more serious consequences. Boxer David

St Mary Street, 1886. The first building on the left of the picture is the Pine Apple Inn.

Lewis lay in a pool of blood on the cobblestones not far from the Philharmonic Hotel after he had been slashed in the throat. Daniel Driscoll, a member of the notorious Cardiff racecourse gang known as 'The Forty Thieves', along with Edward Rowlands, was hanged in Cardiff Prison in 1928 for the murder of Lewis, who had tried to muscle in on their protection racket. Sackfuls of appeal forms were sent to the Home Office and even two members of the jury, which had found Driscoll guilty, went to London to plead for the lives of the two men.

Rowlands had maintained that he alone had killed Lewis while Driscoll wrote home: *'I say I am an innocent man. The evidence against me was so slender that no jury could reasonably find me guilty but for the fact that their minds were inflamed against me by untrue statements.'*

On the morning the two men were executed some 5,000 men, women and children stood outside Cardiff Prison singing hymns. Driscoll, we are told, 'walked proudly to the gallows.' Rowlands, almost unconscious, had to be helped.

Cardiff in the 1840s

A Dr Taylor recalling what Cardiff was like in 1840 had this to say:

'St Mary Street was known as 'The Parish'. There were few houses there. The river [Taff] came right round to the west side of the street and flowed over the spot now occupied by the Royal Hotel. The street at this portion was, in windy weather, a dangerous place to pass because of the tremendous gusts which swept across the moors. I have seen the tide washing over the footpath of St Mary Street and I recollect one fine day seeing a man run across St Mary Street from his house and taking a header into the river.

Mr John Batchelor had a builders yard and slip where he built small vessels, just this side where the Great Western Hotel now stands and which, of course, abutted on the river. The course of the river was not altered to its present bed until the time of the making of the South Wales Railway in 1848. When this took place Mr Batchelor moved his works to the Bute Docks where the Mount Stuart Dry Dock is now.

From the site of the present Hayes Bridge to the south end of St Mary Street, where Millicent Street and Tredegar Street now stand, was open fields.'

Quay Street

T he Quay Street of today bears little resemblance to the Quay Street of 1891. In days of old it was frequented not only by sailors and fishermen, who navigated their crafts to the walls of the old quay, but at one time by the cattlemen who drove their charges to market.

Bull in a Hat Shop

B efore the diverting of the River Taff, vessels unloaded their cargoes in what is now Westgate Street. Sam Allen in his *Reminiscences* has an interesting tale to tell of an incident that took place in Quay Street:

Quay Street – once frequented by sailors and fishermen – 1891.

'At the bottom of Quay Street stood the Slaughter-house, and cattle on their way thither sometimes took it into their heads to stampede, possibly, objecting to the fate waiting them. On one occasion, I saw rather a big crowd outside Mr Richards, the hatter's premises, and desiring of learning the cause of the commotion, pushed my way to the front near the shop door, and then inside the shop, where I beheld a huge bullock at the distant end, with his head down charging a large crate of hats held in front by way of a buffer, in order to protect the manager of the shop, Mr Dykes.

I thought it then time to back out into the street, as there was little room for myself and the bullock. So you can imagine I was not long in mounting the counter, just in time, to see the huge and enraged animal wheel around and make a dart through the open doorway into the fast disappearing crowd in the street.'

The Hayes, c. 1940. The open market held in this area was a flourishing place.

The Hayes

A Mr D. Condren in a letter to the *Cardiff and Suburban News* on 20 January 1945 recalled The Hayes of an earlier time:

'The open market on the Hayes was a flourishing place in bygone days. Scores of barrows and stalls were loaded with goods of every description. Mountebanks, tinkers and peddlers made frequent visits as they wandered along the highway from the market place and fairs in other parts of the country, and much amusement they created. Marionettes, Punch and Judy, sword swallowers, fire eaters and handcuff escapees all gave show on occasions.

The Salvation Army were also there, and it was a pleasure listening to the singing and fervent praying of the members. Great enthusiasm prevailed, and many converts were won over from a worldly to a spiritual state of mind. Appropriately, the spot chosen for their meetings was beneath the shadow of the statue of John Batchelor, 'the Friend of Freedom', a man who lived a good and noble life. With arm extended, the image seemed to look down with a benign benevolence upon those present.

Fruit stalls were prominent, with orchard fruit in season such as apples, pears, plums, grapes, greengages, quinces, gooseberries and damsons. In addition, there were bananas, pineapples, melons, dates, figs, pomegranates, nectarines, tangerines and oranges that were sold two, three and four a penny!

Children would hover about the sweet stalls like butterflies in summer and gaze fondly at the slabs of delicious creamy Devonshire toffee, chunks of coconut icing, marzipan bonbons, sugar plums, humbugs, raspberry drops, pear drops, butterscotch, bull's eyes, aniseed balls and other varieties of old-fashioned confectionery that were sold at four ounces a penny!

There were stalls selling curtains, cast-off clothing, miscellaneous pieces of china and crockery, locust beans, tiger nuts and monkey nuts and even cats' meat. A group of boys would be seen clustered around the glaring fire of a chestnut roaster, and nearby, standing in a carriage, probably hired from the mews for the occasion, a self-styled professor in shining top hat, offering a medicinal mixture which he guaranteed would cure 'all the ills that flesh is heir to'. 'A Harley Street specialist', he exclaims 'would charge five guineas for this prescription, but my fee is a modest sixpence'. With his persuasive patter confidence is soon created, and many bottles are sold and the purchasers are sold too!

An old potter is seen moulding upon his potter's lathe, and a clay-like substance appears readily into the shape of flower pots and other earthenware utensils, the while he discourses with the onlookers upon the beauty of the potter's art.

And behold the Indian chief adorned with head-feathers and face bedabbled with paint. With the help of his squaw he is distributing for a penny a packet which contains a powdered secret root which is guaranteed to whiten and preserve the teeth for a lifetime, in support of which he smiles and displays his own set of gleaming white teeth.

There is a cheerful old fellow, minus a leg, squatting upon a cushion on the pavement, a large canvas spread out before him, upon which is painted a colliery scene. With a stick he points out and describes the various places connected with the mine, after which he sings lustily a song beginning 'Down under the coalmine …' Colliers on holiday from the Welsh coalfields took a keen interest in these proceedings. Many people attended the market to make various purchases; and others to gaze upon the motley sight and enjoy the babble of sounds.'

Charles Vachell

I wonder how many Cardiffians know that Charles Street, in the centre of the city, was named after Charles Vachell who built the first house in the Queen Street area (then known as Crockherbtown). This was sited on land that had been acquired by his father who had run a profitable apothecary in Duke Street. Elected Mayor on two occasions (1849 and 1855) Charles Vachell played a big part in the implementation of the Public Health Act (1848) in Cardiff, because of his concern over the living conditions of some of the people in the town. Despite some

Charles Street, c. 1958. It was named after Charles Vachell, a mayor of Cardiff.

improvements however 1859 saw an epidemic of cholera which killed some 374 Cardiffians.

Fox Hunting from Marks & Spencer

The first mention of Charles Street appears in *Piggot's Street Directory* of 1835. There was a time when a pack of hounds and huntsmen would meet in Charles Street, near where Marks & Spencer is situated now, to go fox hunting.

Open Sewers and Poverty

A local paper dated 10 January 1891, paints a depressing picture of Stanley Street which was situated south of Charles Street:

'Stanley Street, as a street, has no exis-tence. It is almost a cul-de-sac from Bute Terrace, only a few feet wide, having in the centre of it a narrow channel into which is poured all the liquid refuge, slops etc., from the houses on each side. The stench from the lower portion of this open gutter is in summer often abominable. The street, or rather pitched footway, forms the drying ground of the occupants of the houses. A clothes line, common to all, extends from one end of the alley to another and this is in fine weather constantly in use.

In the summer the street forms a kind of

general washhouse and women, in a semi
state of nudity, whose clothes are often
nothing but a collection of dirty rags, with
old earthenware pans placed on broken
chairs, occupy the day.

There are about forty houses in the
street, many consisting of two rooms one
over the other without a back door or an
opening in the wall to give ventilation.
There is scarcely a house with a window
but in which a number of panes of glass are
not broken and the aperture filled with old
rags. There is not a house but in which the
lower half of the outer door is not honey-
combed and large portions eaten away by
rats who in the early morning make the
street and houses a kind of happy hunting
ground for their species.

The bedroom is reached by a staircase
rising from the lower rooms and entering
the upper through an opening in the floor
like a trap door. Police found a woman and
her baby sharing a wooden projection to a
house which sheltered a donkey and homeless children were often found sleeping
under carts.'

This then was Stanley Street only a few
streets away from Charles Street where
the local 'gentry' lived.

Womanby Street, c. 1890. This was the scene of
a battle between pirates in 1759.

'The Battle of Womanby Street'

In Womanby Street in 1759, a fight
took place between the crew of a ship
named *The Eagle of Bristol* and the crew
of a man-o-war called *Aldrough*. The
crews were armed to the teeth with pis-
tols, swords, pikes, cutlasses and mus-
kets. At the end of the battle, one man
lay dead and many were wounded. The
affair being nobody's business, apart

from the ships' crews, was hushed up
and a coroner's court declared that the
deceased sailor, Edmund Ffaharty, had
been shot 'by persons unknown'.

The Horse and Groom pub in
Womanby Street was once known
as the Red Cow and it was from there
that the Cardiff to Cowbridge coach
would start. Womanby Street has also
been known as Hundemanby (c. 1270),
Houndemammeby (1310), Homandesby
(1432), Whomanby (1550), Homanby
(1600) and Howmanby (1716). The
name is thought to mean 'the home or
dwelling of the hound man or keeper of
hounds'.

The Three Horse Shoes in High Street, 1890.

Shebeens, Drinking Dens and Inns

Between the years 1850 and 1875 some 92 licensed premises could be found in central Cardiff. There were also illegal drinking houses which were known as 'shebeens'. These back-street drinking dens, in which ale was served in the front room of little terraced houses, accounted for a large proportion of the beer that was sold in the town. Licences to sell beer were hard to come by and these beer-shop owners were often prosecuted for 'holding a shebeen'.

In those days Charlotte Street, which branched off from Bute Street and led to St Mary Street, was known as 'The Street of Taverns'. It had in all twelve inns: The Ship, The Six Bells, Britannia, Caledonian, Irishman's Glory, King's Head, Duke of Gloucester, Farmer's Arms, Excavator's Arms, Seven Stars, Red Lion and Dinas Arms. And just for good measure [pardon the pun] there was also a beer and porter stores.

The Canal Bank at the rear of Charlotte Street housed the Tunnel Tavern, Dunraven Castle and Hills Arms Tavern while in nearby Caroline Street could be found the Cambrian Arms, Neptune, Bristol Arms, Loyal Windsor and Victoria. The Franklyn, Scandinavian, Inkerman, Wexford & Kinsale, Plume of Feathers, Elephant & Castle and several others could be found in Bute Terrace. In Bridge Street there was a pub called The Beehive which was kept by a Mrs Hole. As an open invitation to enter her pub there was a notice in the window which read: 'In This Hive We Are All Alive. Good Liquor Makes Us Funny, So If You Are Dry, Step Inside And Try The Flavour Of Our Honey'.

One of the most popular public houses in the centre of Cardiff was the old Rose and Crown and despite a campaign to get it listed by the Welsh Office, along with the old cobbled courtyard at the rear of the building, it was demolished in 1974 to make way for another pub of the same name which has recently been renamed Coopers. The Rose and Crown had its Kingsway (North Street) location on the east side of the North Gate of the town as early as 1787.

Another of the oldest inn sites in town is that occupied by the Owain Glyndwr in Church Street. Apparently in 1731 it was known as the Mably Arms and later as the Kemeys-Tynte Arms. In the 1950s it was known as The Tennis Courts and became The Buccaneer sometime afterwards.

The Black Lion and The Angel, The Griffin and The White Lion

The Black Lion, later known as the Sandringham, which stood for generations in St Mary Street, and the Angel Hotel were the two principal hotels in Cardiff. They were much frequented by the farmers of Glamorgan and Monmouthshire especially on mar-

ket days. The local fairs were then held in the streets and the old market place occupied a position at the rear of the Town Hall in the centre of High Street.

The old Black Lion was, according to a Mr Charles Evans, who wrote a series of letters to a local paper about the pubs of his day and from whom much of this information has been obtained, '*a house of entertainment for man and beast and many a Cardiff tradesman of the old school and several salts of the then small port of the River Taff were wont to congregate at the hostelry in the evening and take their ease at that inn*'.

Near the site of the present market once stood the Griffin Inn. This house adjoined the county prison and when a prisoner had been sent down the expres-

British Volunteer Hotel, The Hayes, c. 1890.

Stevens & Son Wine & Spirit Merchants, High Street, 1874.

sion 'Gone next-door to the Griffin' was a well-known one. The other Griffin, which will be known to some Cardiffians, stood on the other side of St Mary Street by where the National Westminster Bank now stands. It was built upon the site of the old Cardiff Playhouse.

The Angel Hotel (later Bute Offices) was the inn at which the London coach stopped and changed horses. The Cardiff Arms near the site of the present Angel Hotel jutted out into Cowbridge Road facing the castle. Nearly opposite the old Cardiff Arms, facing the corner

of a row of shops which stood in the centre of Broad Street, was the Cowbridge Arms. Between the old bridge over the Taff and Cardiff Castle and nearly facing the Cardiff Arms on the Castle side of the road stood the ancient Five Bells.

A little further on nearer town on the same side of the road as the Five Bells was the White Lion, built right on the Castle wall. The White Lion was a busy house on market days it being a place where farmers coming to town from the west side put up their horses and conveyances. On the other side of the street

Masons Arms Hotel, Queen Street. It stood between 1795 and 1920. The post-box is believed to have been the first in Cardiff.

Royal Hotel and old houses, west side of St Mary Street, c. 1870.

from the old Angel Hotel was Ty Derwen (Fair Oak House).

In the centre of Queen Street and running from the corner of St Johns Square to the canal in Crockherbtown was a block of buildings which divided Queen Street into two streets. This place was known as Running Camp where the popular inn Carey's Place was situated.

The Animal Wall

In 1883 Lord Bute gave orders that the wall in front of Cardiff Castle should be mounted by animal figures. There were long and detailed discussions as to the size and choice of the animals and it wasn't until some five years later in 1888 that his instructions were finally completed.

The *Western Mail*, dated 26 September 1888, told its readers:

'The beauty of the approach to Cardiff on the Canton side has been enhanced by the erection in front of the Castle of an ornate wall, broken up with a recessed hammered railing of an exquisite design which enables passers-by to obtain a complete view of the grounds lying round the forepart of the Castle. Quite a new departure has been

This stone bear is said to have replaced the original polar bear in the Animal Wall outside Cardiff Castle.

taken in outside decoration.

The rough stones were sent to the studio of Mr Nicholls, a well-known London sculptor, to be carved into various forms of animal life, and the first two to leave the sculptor's hands were bedded on Wednesday in the masonry and were objects of a good deal of interest. They represent a life-size seal and a large female baboon nursing its offspring. In all a dozen different mammals adorn the coping of the wall'.

William Rees in his *Cardiff – A History of the City* informs us that the first models included a sea-lion, monkeys and possibly a sea-horse and a pelican. The original lions 'were deemed to be modest in demeanour, savouring rather as pets than of roaring lions and were later returned for re-touching'. The animals were moved to their present site in 1928 when figures of a vulture, a beaver, a

The retouched lions (left and above).

leopard, a pelican, raccoons and an anteater were added along with a bear which replaced the original polar bear. Some of them are said to have been executed by Mr Nicholls' son – his model of the bear came in for a lot of praise – and by a Mr William Antrill who was probably sub-contracted to Mr Nicholls.

Rita Spurr, writing in *The Lady* in 1959, claims that the vulture, beaver, leopard, ant eater and raccoons were not added until 1931 and that they were the work of Alexander Carrick RSA, of Edinburgh. Be that as it may, it is certain that for many years to come the animals will be a feature of interest and amusement to thousands of Cardiffians and visitors to Cardiff.

34), which featured a Georgian façade and a double flight of stone steps flanked by an ironwork balustrade, was opened in 1747.

With the increase in the population in the days when 'Coal was King' and the subsequent opening of the Bute Docks, it soon became clear that a much larger town hall was needed. An acre of land between St Mary Street and Westgate Street – where the Commercial Bank of Wales now stands – was put aside and building commenced in 1849. During the work earlier walls were found and a circular stairway of great depth, thought to be part of the old town's defences, was also uncovered. Opened in 1854, the new town hall also housed the old post office, police court and parade ground, as well

The hyena (above) and the lynx (right).

Town Halls

Cardiff's first town hall, which was also known as the Town House, Bothall or Guildhall, was erected halfway along High Street in 1331. A two-storey building, the upper floor served as a court room and general assembly room. On the ground floor could be found the prison cells, stocks, water pump and the corn and meat markets, which were known as the 'Shambles'.

A turret, town bell and clock tower were added much later but by 1741 the building was in such a bad state of repair that a decision was made to build another town hall on the same site. This new building (pictured on page

When the animal wall stood in front of Cardiff Castle, c. 1900.

The old Town Hall in High Street was used from 1747 until 1860.

as the fire brigade offices and rates office.

The Building of the City Hall

At a meeting of the council of the County Borough of Cardiff on 6 December 1897 it was resolved: '*to empower the Corporation to erect and maintain in the said park (Cathays) a Town Hall*'. On that day competitive designs were on display in the assembly room of the old Town Hall and a few days later Mr Alfred Waterhouse RA, acting as competition assessor to the fifty-six architects whose designs had been put forward, awarded the first prize of £500 to Lanchester, Stewart and Rickards of London.

Six years later, during the first half of 1900, work commenced when a dwarf wall and railings were constructed around a one-acre site of Cathays Park. John Kyte Collett, an architect, had

The new Town Hall, 1854.

Town Hall, St Mary Street, c. 1915.

Workmen taking a break during the building of the City Hall, c. 1903.

Laying the foundation stone of City Hall, 23 October 1901.

drawn up plans for the proposed new Town Hall to be built in Temperance Town. It was no surprise to find that he was one of twenty-six local owners and ratepayers who signed a deputation urging that the building of the new Town Hall be postponed for a few years.

Excavation work for the foundations of the Town Hall and the Law Courts took over twelve months. However, 1901 saw the foundations being laid and on 23 October at 12 noon the Marquess of Bute and the Mayor of Cardiff,

Councillor Thomas Andrews, who had been instrumental in the introduction of trams, free libraries and the new civic centre, performed the ceremony.

Top-hatted dignitaries were grouped under a ceremonial awning as the great block of Portland stone swung down by a cable from a crane. The Marquess, coming forward with a spirit level and a mallet, declared it well and truly laid. A Cardiff photographer, Alfred Freke, who had been granted permission to take the pictures, photographed the great occa-

Rear view of City Hall before the Welsh National War Memorial was built.

City Hall, c. 1906.

Modern-day picture of City Hall. The Welsh National War Memorial can be seen directly behind the clock tower.

sion for posterity.

Almost three years later, the capstone of the tower was placed in position and in October 1906, a year after Cardiff had been granted City status, the City Hall buildings were formally declared open by Lord Bute. The stone which had been quarried in the Forest of Dean had come down on carts pulled by great shire horses.

Herbert House

There are still many Cardiffians who can remember the ruins of Herbert House which used to be in Greyfriars Road. I can remember standing on the wall, which surrounded the gardens and looking through the iron railings at the ruins of this once historic house when I was a young lad in the 1950s. John Ballinger, in his *Guide to Cardiff* (published in 1908), writes:

'The Grey Friars (Franciscans or Friars Minors) had their house in

The ruins of Herbert House in Greyfriars Road, c. 1940.

Crockherbtown, south of the new City Hall. After the dissolution the site was acquired by Sir George Herbert, whose grandson, Sir William, built a mansion known as The Friars, a portion of which is still standing, a light handsome structure in Tudor style. The site of the Grey Friars Church was excavated by the Marquis of Bute who had the outlines rebuilt to a few feet above the ground. Some graves inside the church were discovered and marked. It was here that Llewellin Bren and his foe, Sir William Fleming, were buried but attempts to identify the graves were not satisfactory.'

The Cruel Death of Llywelyn Bren

The remains of Llewellin Bren (or Llywelyn Bren) were said to be carried to Grey Friars for a Christian burial in 1317 after he had been dragged to a traitor's death for his part in a short-lived Welsh revolt. The Welsh chieftain was allegedly put to death at Cardiff with great barbarity and in direct violation of the King's command. He was drawn by horses, then hanged, his entrails taken out and burned while his limbs were cut off 'and sent through the whole of Glamorgan, to strike terror into other traitors.'

As for Sir William Fleming, when fortunes changed he was hanged at Cardiff Castle's Black Tower. His tomb, which was made of fair stone, and Llywelyn Bren's tomb, said to be made of wood, were apparently still in Grey Friars Church when it was dismantled in 1538. And they were thought to have

been discovered in 1887 along with the skeletons of men, women and children on the site where the monstrous Pearl Assurance tower block now stands. It was a great shame when this historic landmark and holy site was demolished in the 1960s to make way for a building which, to coin a cliché, stands out like a sore thumb!

Cardiff Central Library

The old Central Library in Trinity Street served Cardiff people well for more than a century. It owed its beginnings to a local architect Mr Peter Price who wrote to the Cardiff and Merthyr Guardian on a number of occasions advocating the adoption of the Free Libraries Act of 1855.

In 1861 a voluntary library was set up in a reading room above the entrance to the Royal Arcade in St Mary Street. The following year – 1862 – the acts were implemented and Cardiff became the first local authority in the Principality to adopt them and provide a public library.

After much argument and discussion, the Corporation resolved in 1879 that Trinity Street would be the site for the Free Library, Museum and Schools of Art and Science. On 27 October 1880 the foundation stone was laid by the Mayor John McConnochie and placed within the cavity of the stone were copies of the local newspapers of that date along with a specimen of each coin of the realm.

On 31 May 1882 Mayor Alfred Thomas declared the northern end of the library open. There was much

Opening of the Central Library extension in Trinity Street, 1896.

rejoicing with processions and other festivities which ended with a social
evening in the Town Hall.

The southern extension was opened
by the Prince of Wales, later King
Edward VII, in 1896. He was accompanied by his wife Princess Alexandra and
their daughters the Princesses Maud and
Victoria. The new large reading room
was the scene of the opening ceremony
where the Prince gave a speech and was
presented with a golden key to com-
memorate the occasion. His wife was
presented with a copy of John
Ballinger's *History of Cardiff Free Library*.
A magnificent fireworks display at
Sophia Gardens ended the day's proceedings.

Cardiff writer Jack Jones, a former
coal-miner, made good use of the library
in the late 1940s and early 1950s spending countless hours reading back copies
of the *Western Mail* and other local
newspapers when researching material
for his novels: *River Out Of Eden, Black
Diamond, Bidden To The Feast* and *Off
To Philadelphia In The Morning*.

He later wrote: '*I always feel most
grateful for the great privilege of yet another
glimpse of its riches, riches of which the
majority of those whom the library serves
are seemingly unaware … I believe that the
vision that redeemed Cardiff from what it
was to what it is now, a fine city in almost*

every respect, with a civic centre as impressive as it is unique in the world today ... was born in the Cardiff Library on a day in the 'Nineties when Edward the Prince of Wales performed the opening ceremony'.

John Ballinger, whose statue once stood just outside the southern side of the building, was appointed librarian in 1884. He resigned in 1908 to become chief librarian at the National Library of Wales in Aberystwyth. The new Cardiff and County Council Library in Frederick Street was opened in 1987.

The National War Memorial

The Welsh National War Memorial, which stands in the centre of Alexandra Gardens, was unveiled by Edward, Prince of Wales, on 12 June 1928. Its main features are the three bronze statues of a sailor, a soldier and an airman. Lloyd George said of this magnificent Romanesque Portland stone memorial that it was 'exquisite'.

Over the years many hundreds of people must have gazed up at the three servicemen and wondered whether they were posed for and, if so, by whom. One would have thought that the statues were based on three real Welsh servicemen. However, the statue of the sailor

Left: Fred Baker posing for the sailor in the studio.

Right: the bronze figure of the sailor that Fred Baker posed for.

42

The Welsh National War Memorial. Who posed for the soldier and airman?

was, in fact, modelled on a Londoner! His name was Frederick William Baker, and he was born in Brixton on 9 October 1897. At the age of 17 he joined the Royal Navy and his service record tells that he served on many ships and stations including the *Vivid*, *Powerful*, *Roxburgh*, *Repulse*, *Pembroke*, *Ambrose*, *Tarantula* and *Courageous*.

When I was co-ordinator of the now defunct City Hall-based Historic Records Project, around ten years ago, I received a visit from a Mrs Patricia Jeffries who lived near London. She had never visited Cardiff before and the purpose of her journey was to see and obtain some information on this fine memorial. As it happened one could see the memorial from my office window, but nevertheless I escorted her to the actual place and it was then that she told me a most remarkable story. Her father, Frederick William Baker, in uniform, was coming out of Waterloo Station, London, when a man ran up to him and said: 'You have the very face I have been looking for'. The complete stranger turned out to be Mr A.E. Burton, of Thames Ditton, who was responsible for the bronze castings of the three servicemen on the memorial and he explained to the somewhat surprised sailor that he had already found the men to pose for the soldier and airmen and that he wanted him to depict the sailor.

An emotional Mrs Jeffries, looking up at the memorial for the first time, told me she was proud that her father had been chosen to represent the Welsh sailor and that he had died in 1962. She later sent me a photograph of her father posing for Mr Burton and I was able to send her some more information on the Welsh National War Memorial. One thing I couldn't tell her though were the names of the two men who posed for the statues of the soldier and airman. Perhaps we will never know now.

CHAPTER 2

Sport, leisure and entertainment

Sophia Gardens Lodge which was bombed during the Second World War.

Sophia Gardens Lodge

The Sophia Gardens Lodge, which used to stand opposite where the City Temple is now situated, was bombed on 3 March 1941. One Cardiffian who remembers that dreadful evening is Mr Malcolm Beames. He recalled: *'We were in a public air-raid shelter near Sophia Gardens when all of a sudden there was a tremendous explosion and we heard later on that the park keeper, who lived in the lodge, had been killed'*.

Sophia Gardens, named after Sophia, the second wife of the Marquess of Bute, was opened in 1858. There used to be an attractive drinking fountain there and over the years the grounds have been the venue for flower shows, horse shows, concerts, cricket matches and various other sports events and occasions.

Roath Park

Roath Park was opened to the public on 20 June 1894. The day's festivities began with a luncheon at the Town Hall to which some 300 people had been invited. At the appointed time, the various trade organisations, friendly societies and local bodies equipped with bands and banners and in many cases wearing the regulation uniform of their order, or bearing artistic models of their crafts, assembled at Cardiff Arms Park where thousands of spectators had already gathered to witness the proceedings.

The Boilermakers' and Ship Builders' Union of South Wales decorated their lorries with gigantic specimens of their skill and workmanship. Most of the men, the *Cardiff Times* informed its readers, *'wore buttonholes or rosettes and seemed to enjoy themselves to the utmost'*.

The Sophia Gardens fountain was in place in 1866. The boy is Snowden Pearson who later became a well-known Cardiff dentist.

Sheepdog trials, Sophia Gardens, c. 1950.

The Cardiff Hibernians, who followed in the wake of the engineers, presented a highly creditable turn-out; their silk hats, white trousers and regalia evoked no end of favourable comment from the thousands of people who lined the route.

Special trains had been laid on from Swansea, Bristol and the Valleys and for a couple of hours prior to the opening ceremony the main thoroughfares leading to the park entrance were crowded with heavily laden buses, tram cars and private conveyances all making their way to the park.

The procession through town extending from St Mary Street to Roath Park was one unbroken line. Albany Road and Wellfield Road in particular presented a very animated appearance. Streamers and flags were suspended across the streets at intervals and the tremendous crush of people in holiday attire helped to make the scene one of lively anticipation.

The music of the various bands announced the arrival of the procession and members of the Corporation alighted from their carriages. Contractor Mr James Allan handed the chairman of the parks committee a gold key which he in turn handed to the Mayor who, with a few well-chosen words, presented it to the young Earl of Dumfries who that very day was celebrating his thirteenth birthday.

The party then proceeded to the platform and was greeted by a round of applause from the spectators. The town clerk proceeded to read the address to the Earl of Dumfries, which the Mayor, Alderman Trounce, subsequently presented to him. In a brief reply the Earl, addressing the assembled crowd in both English and Welsh, declared Roath Park open for the use of the public.

Cardiff Horse Show, Sophia Gardens, c. 1950.

Gymkhana at Cardiff Horse Show, Sophia Gardens, c. 1950.

48

Roath Park Lake, c. 1920.

Over the years Roath Park has been the scene of numerous concerts, regattas, water carnivals, dance nights, Punch and Judy shows and all sorts of other attractions. In Edwardian times as many as 2,000 people could be seen swimming in the lake on Sunday mornings. In those days, the ladies and gentlemen had their own bathing sections as mixed bathing was not allowed.

Mrs Kath Davies recalled that during the Second World War her father, Tom Davies, organised 'Holidays at Home' in Roath Park. Open-air dancing in one short summer attracted 50,000 people to the park. She reminisced:
'I can well remember the various competitions when parents were given a roll of crêpe paper and produced a fancy dress on the spot. A very personal memory is being taken on the paddle boats named after the Seven Dwarfs and being teased by my brothers because mine was called Dopey'.

Mr Keith Bennett from Fairwater recalled: *'My parents used to take me there in the 1930s and I enjoyed riding the many-seated rocking horse'.* Miss Phyllis Carey, of Roath, remembers the fireworks displays and the hymn singing that used to take place in the park before the last war: *'It's a funny thing, but I don't remember it ever raining'.*

When swimming was allowed in Roath Park lake, c. 1925. Joan 'Girlie' Donovan is to the left and Mamie Burge, right.

Victoria Park – the Beginnings

On 21 January 1891 the Corporation's Property Committee decided to transfer to the Park Committee a part of Ely Common for the purpose of a park. This portion of land, of almost 20 acres, was known during the early stages of its construction as Ely Common Park or just Ely Park.

The future Victoria Park first received the consideration of the Parks Committee on 16 June 1891 when alternative plans were submitted by Mr Harpur the Borough Engineer for laying out that portion of Ely Common for recreation purposes.

Mr Harpur explained that it would be for the committee to decide whether there would be a lake in the park, but he feared the ground was too porous. The committee decided to defer consideration until the Public Works Council

Children paddling, Roath Park, c. 1896.

Gymnastic display, Roath Park, c. 1948.

had extended the Cowbridge Road sewer to the common, by which means it was intended to drain the new park. There followed a row between the Property Committee and Parks Committee as to the spending of the balance of £8,362 still remaining. However, this was settled at a council meeting on 9 October 1893. A few days before this the Borough Engineer had submitted to a joint meeting of the Parks and Property Committees, an estimate of £7,747 as the cost of fencing and laying out Ely Common as a pleasure ground.

Victoria Park was 'thrown open to the public' on Wednesday 16 June 1897. The ceremony was performed by the Mayor, who was accompanied by nearly all the members of the Corporation. 'As *might have been expected, Canton was "en fête" for it was a red letter day in the popu-lous district. While the other districts of Cardiff have had open spaces provided for the delectation of the public, Canton has had to wait. Now, however, their turn has come. A fine new park of 20 acres the portion of that old-time swamp known as Ely Common. It is a beautifully laid out piece of ground with smooth firm greenswards and broad laid paths, and delightful beds well furnished with flowers, shrubs and trees. There is a lake with two beautiful fountains in it, there is a substantial and yet artistic bandstand, and a 2 acre space of playground for the children'.*

A Tank in Victoria Park

On 6 May 1919 the Parks Committee accepted a gift of a tank and it was decided to place it in

Youngsters enjoying a dip in Victoria Park's paddling pool, c. 1950.

Victoria Park on a spot adjoining Cowbridge Road. The Lord Mayor, Councillor A.C. Kirk and members of the Corporation assembled at Victoria Park on 2 June 1919 and Major E.L. Williams, Officer Commanding Welch Regiment, on behalf of the National War Savings Committee asked the Lord Mayor to accept the tank as a permanent record of the patriotism and self sacrifice of the people of Cardiff. At one time two captured German field artillery guns also went to Victoria Park.

First World War Rationing at Victoria Park

On 6 June 1917 it was reported that the average weekly cost of food for the animals at Victoria Park was £4 19s 0d. This included 34 shillings for fish for the seal.

It was felt that apart from the difficulty of obtaining supplies the cost of feeding 'Billy' was proving prohibitive. A sub-committee was formed 'to report as the best course to adopt with regard the seal'. One suggestion put forward was that 'Billy' be returned to the sea. It was eventually resolved that 'he' be put on half rations for one month and that the chairman be authorized to destroy the seal if, in his opinion, he should consider it advisable. 'Billy' survived on half rations thanks to his public admirers whose tit-bits kept 'him' going until the end of the war.

Breeding Rabbits for Food

On 7 March 1918, the chief officer submitted a letter from Mr Leigh Jones, Director of Messrs R.E. Jones Ltd, offering on behalf of Mr H. Stevens (Leicester) and himself to assist the Corporation in the event of their deciding to undertake the breeding of rabbits as a means of increasing food supplies. The committee accepted and left the matter to a sub-committee and authorized them to spend £10 on stock. The last of the rabbit breeding is mentioned in the proceedings of the Parks Committee on 4 December 1918 when the chief officer authorized the advertisement of twenty rabbits for sale.

Billy the Seal

On display in the National Museum of Wales in Cardiff can be seen a skeleton of what was once a common grey seal. But this particular seal was no ordinary creature and more that fifty years after its death in 1939, Billy is still fondly remembered by many Cardiffians and BBC Radio Wales's Frank Hennessy has immortalised Cardiff's most famous animal in song.

Accidentally caught off the Irish

The legendary Billy the Seal, c. 1930.

coast in the net of a Neale and West fishing boat in 1912, Billy was placed in a box of fish and later discovered by a woman buying fish for her market stall.

Billy was presented to Cardiff Corporation and was placed in Victoria Park Lake which in those days was much larger and deeper and surrounded by railings and bushes. Billy soon became the star attraction of the park's small zoo which also housed peacocks, goats, parrots, gazelles, monkeys and a few other animals.

One Cardiffian, Mrs Valentine Tucker, recalled:

'There would be rows of children lining the railways around the pool, calling "Billy! Billy!" until he came snorting and wide-eyed out of the depths. I was always amazed that he could hear our voices from under the water. Making scarcely a ripple he would come close to the edge to look at us, his round, brilliant eyes alive with interest.

Children tossed him sweets or biscuits or unwanted picnic sandwiches which he did not even bother to investigate but, occasionally, one of the children would have acquired a couple of herring heads or cod guttings, and on these occasions Billy always knew. Not that he needed a particular sensitive sense of smell for such titbits. They had usually been clasped for some time in hot young hands and the all-pervading odour could be identified at some distance. Heading for the place where the child stood, with radar-like accuracy, and to our combined cries of "Over, Bill, Over", he would roll over for us, uttering little cries of anticipation.'

Another reminisced:

'A visit to Victoria Park in those days to see Billy the Seal was considered a great treat. Children would regularly walk from Penarth and Barry and en route to the park would stop at fishmongers to buy scraps for Billy who would leap up to catch the fish and tumble about and generally rollick around as the life and soul of the party.'

When Victoria Park and most of the surrounding area was flooded in 1927, Billy escaped and was found boarding a tram in Cowbridge Road. The story goes that the conductor told Billy to roll over and Billy rolled back into the flooded road. Other reports had Billy sighted in several fish and chip shops and even visiting a dentist! So many people have claimed that Billy ended up on their front doors one can only envisage that Billy visited nearly everyone in Canton!

Attempts were made to provide Billy with a companion. In 1917 a female seal was introduced to Billy, but it sadly died a month or so later. Then in 1926 a small bull seal, which had been washed up at Pendine, was placed in the lake but it didn't survive very long either. Another seal, this time a female, was placed in the lake in 1934 and just like the others it did not live very long.

Billy, however, continued to amuse and entertain visitors to Victoria Park for 27 years until 'he' was found dead by a park keeper at the bottom of the lake in 1939. It has been said that it took eight men to lift Billy out of the water, little wonder considering the amount of titbits Billy had been fed over the years. The body was taken to the National Museum of Wales where it was discovered that 'he' was in fact a 'she'! This discovery led to some speculation that perhaps this particular seal was an impostor. The original male 'Billy', it was said, might have died or escaped and had been replaced by a female seal. But to thousands of Cardiffians, with happy memories of visiting Victoria Park in their childhood, there will always be only one Billy the Seal.

Maindy Pool, 1928.

Stadia: Cardiff Arms Park

It goes without saying that Cardiff's best-known stadium is the Cardiff Arms Park – these days known as the National Stadium and currently being rebuilt in time for the 1999 World Rugby Cup. The first rugby international played there was in 1884 when Wales beat Ireland. Cicket was also played there for many years.

However, perhaps the biggest sporting occasion to have taken place at the Cardiff Arms Park was the 1958 Empire and Commonwealth Games.

Maindy Stadium

Maindy Stadium was built on the site of an old clay pit known as Maindy Pool. Believed to be 65 feet deep in parts, several adults and at least nine children were drowned there. Between 1926 and 1934, however, some 16,000 cart loads of rubbish were tipped into its waters in order to prepare the site for the stadium.

This was opened in 1951, but only

Workers construct the terraces of Maindy Stadium with stones taken from the Glamorgan Canal, c. 1949.

the cycle track, which at one time was one of the best in the world, remains. The legendary cyclist Reg Harris raced there and Cardiff's Don Skene won a bronze medal at Maindy in the 1958 Empire and Commonwealth Games.

In the 1960s at Maindy, Welshman Lynn Hughes became the first man in the world to run 40 miles on the track inside four hours and for many years the Welsh AAA Championships were staged there. I recall the legendary Welsh heavyweight boxer Tommy Farr fighting at Maindy in the early 1950s. My father was in charge of the water buckets and I was helping him.

The Harlequins Ground

The Harlequins ground off Newport Road has a much longer history. In 1894 the first Mallet Rugby Cup final was played there. Around 1,000 spectators saw Cardiff Reserves beat Canton. In 1897 the Welsh Cross Country Championships took place there and the course was a most difficult one. It included 22 water jumps ranging from 8 feet wide to 22 feet wide. Cardiff Harriers won but it was a Newport Harrier, A. Turner, who was first home.

Professional athletics were also held there and the famed Cardiff runner Harry Cullum challenged London's Bredin to a match over 1,000 yards for £100 a side. Cullum won easily in 2 minutes and 20 seconds over a very heavy grass track.

Another well-known Cardiff runner

Start of the 1958 Welsh Marathon Championship at Maindy Stadium. Author Brian Lee is in fifth place with 26 miles to go!

of the time was R.C. Brookes and in 1895 he won the mile at Cardiff Harlequins sports beating former champion Kibblewhite by half a lap. He won so easily that the promoters withheld his prize for a fortnight! That same year he won a 4-mile handicap race over the course and later a 10-mile scratch race at Sophia Gardens. In 1898 he proved himself to be the best runner in Wales when winning the Welsh Cross Country Championship at Ely Racecourse.

Tredegarville Racing Track

Where the Cardiff Royal Infirmary now stands was once the Tredegarville Racing Track later known as the Cardiff Bycycle Ground. In 1897 David Stanton, the English penny farthing cycling champion challenged Welsh champion G.T. Edmunds of Swansea to a 50-mile race for £25 a side. The record then stood at 3 hours and 6 minutes and the organisers promised a sum of £20 if this was beaten. The ground was packed to capacity and although Edmunds was given a 2-mile start, he was caught and passed before the 20-mile mark. Stanton's winning time of 2 hours and 59 minutes was a new world record and when he revealed to the crowd that he was originally from Breconshire they cheered him even more.

Mick Holland, a great favourite with Cardiff speedway fans.

Grangetown Stadium

Before the First World War Grangetown Stadium, situated on the lower end of Clive Street, was the scene of whippet racing, professional sprinting and galloway horse racing.

It was at the Grangetown Stadium back in 1919 that two Cardiff bookmakers invented the 'Electric Judge' which may have been the forerunner of today's computerised timing system. The bookies H. Duggan and a Mr Dywer, who were sports promoters at the track, installed the 'Electric Judge' at the stadium. They claimed it gave results within a fraction of an inch and had worked well during its trial period at the stadium. Each competitor had to run through a gate at the end of his lane and break the tape. This broke an electrical contact and the sprinter's number would fall into place on the indicating board in the position in which he finished.

The Sloper Road Stadium in Grangetown was known as the Welsh White City and the Welsh Greyhound Derby was staged there from 1928 until 1937. It was in the August of 1930 that the legendary greyhound Mick the Miller set a world record in the semifinal of the Welsh Greyhound Derby clocking 29.60 seconds. 'Mick' who won 19 consecutive races, beat his own record in the final a week later when he clocked 29.55 seconds.

Cardiff Dragons Speedway Team

Speedway motorcycle racing first came to Cardiff in the 1920s and was held at the Sloper Road Stadium which closed during the war years. The sport returned in 1951 to Penarth Road Stadium, said to be one of the best tracks in the country. Thousands of Cardiff Dragons fans (I was one of them) would flock to Penarth Road Stadium on Thursday nights to cheer home their favourite riders like Mick Holland, Chum Taylor and Kevin Hayden. Hayden was the first Cardiff rider to hold the track record and was also the first 'Dragon' to score a league maximum number of points.

One of the best meetings was in 1952 when Cardiff Dragons entertained Plymouth. That evening the track

Penarth Road Speedway Stadium, 1952.

Cardiff Dragons speedway team.

record was broken no fewer than five times and the Dragons beat Plymouth 47 to 37. Teams from Sweden, New Zealand and America raced there when the World Championships took place the same year.

When The Walking Boom Hit Cardiff

The heel and toe boom came to Cardiff in 1903 with professions like hairdressers, accountants, photographers, coal merchants and printers all staging their own road walks. One of the biggest events was the Cardiff to Porthcawl Walking Race.

One morning in June 1903 some 57 competitors lined up at 7 a.m. outside the Angel Hotel. They were dressed in white canvas hats, white flannel singlets and navy blue or white shorts. Thousands had gathered to watch the start and a local newspaper of the time reveals: 'There were motor cars of Oxo and Bovril, gaily decorated and equipped with delicacies such as champagne, rice puddings, bananas and other fruit. Also there was a man with a cinematograph to secure films for exhibition at the Empire Theatre'. Cabs, traps, waggonettes and vehicles of every description were laden with people who had resolved to follow the event at their leisure. When the walkers started they were followed by mounted police to see that they were not interfered with.

The finish was at the Esplanade Hotel and first to break the tape, after leading almost throughout, was 22-year-old Roy Thomas, of Messrs Perch &

Company. He took just over 4 hours and 37 minutes for the 28-mile journey and on his way had Oxo and champagne for refreshment!

When the wooden-legged fraternity of Cardiff and District held their walk some 30,000 people lined the route. The course was from the Rose & Crown, Kingsway, to the fourth milestone in Whitchurch. It is reported that there were 15,000 people at the start to cheer the 'peg-leg' competitors on their way. The winner in 47 minutes and 20 seconds was W. Pople from Grangetown who received a tremendous ovation. He finished nearly three minutes ahead of another Cardiffian, Mr A. Collier.

Six Western Mail linotype operators, after working all night, walked from the Royal Oak in Broadway to Newport and finished in the following order: Bert Hill, J.P. Pryse, Frank Morgan, Alec Davies, Alec Crafter and Fred Morgan. The winner took 1 hour and 56 minutes for the 10-mile trip.

Mixed pool, Guildford Crescent Swimming Baths, c. 1948.

Guildford Crescent Swimming Baths

In 1896 the Lady Mayoress Lady Windsor opened to the public the new Guildford Crescent Swimming Baths. Like thousands of other Cardiffians I learned to swim there as a young schoolboy. And I still have the certificate to prove it! As kids we spent most of Saturday mornings jumping from the top of the diving table at the baths and shouting out 'Geronimo' as

we plunged into six feet of water. I think it was sixpence to get in. We changed in a box with a kind of stable door and our clothes had to be put in boxes fastened to the wall. My pal Keith had his underpants stolen on one occasion and he was afraid to go home as he knew he would get a hiding from his mum!

After we were told to get out of the water we would put a penny in the Brylcreem machine for a dollop of that creamy substance made famous by cricketer Dennis Compton.

Changing boxes, Guildford Crescent Swimming Baths, c. 1948.

Coffee machine, Guildford Crescent Swimming Baths, c. 1950.

Before the First World War, one of the star attractions at the various swimming exhibitions staged at the baths was Miss Kitty Slight, a member of the Cardiff Ladies' Swimming Club. Billed as 'Cardiff's Youngest Swimmer', little Kitty, who couldn't have been more than four years old, endeared herself to the spectators with her skilful swimming act. She was coached by a Professor Michael who also trained two other small girls, Miss Iona and her sister Bonnie, described as 'Cardiff's Little Water Queens'.

'The Bars', as we kids used to call them, provided endless hours of fun for generations of Cardiff children. It was used by countless children and adults, swimming clubs, serious swimmers and fun swimmers alike for more than a hundred years (the original Guildford Swimming Baths was opened in 1862).

Ely Racecourse grandstands, c. 1925.

But despite petitions to keep it open, it was closed in 1984 and demolished the following year to make way for a car park.

Cardiff's Vanished Racecourse

The sport of kings is believed to have first come to Ely on 30 May 1855. However, horse racing was not entirely new to the Cardiff area for there had been an old racecourse at Heath Farm in which Cardiff Corporation had taken a lively interest. Ely Racecourse owed its beginnings to the sporting land owners and hunting folk of Glamorgan, such as the Homfrays, the Williamses, the Lewises, the Lindsays and the Copes who were later to form the nucleus of the Cardiff Race Club.

There was a time when Cardiff was without horse racing and the *South Wales Daily News*, dated 29 April 1886, reported that: '*After an interval of eight years Cardiff was on Wednesday once more the scene of racing, and judging from the amount of public interest taken in the proceedings, there would appear to be good ground for believing that, if not for all time, at any rate for a long time to come, the inhabitants of the Welsh metropolis may look to the annual recurrence of the event*'.

In fact, Ely Racecourse was to survive right up until the start of the Second World War. Aintree Grand National winners Cloister, Father O'Flynn, Golden Miller and the famed Brown Jack are just a few of the equine stars to have graced the Ely turf.

Shortly before he died, the legendary trainer Fulke Walwyn told me: '*I had my first ride under National Hunt rules at Cardiff and luckily for me it turned out to be a winner. The horse's name was Alpine Hunt and I won a two-mile novice chase on him. He turned out to be a very useful*

63

Members crossing from the enclosure to the paddock, c. 1925.

Winning jockey David Thomas with the 1926 Welsh Grand National winner Miss Balscadden.

Miss Balscadden (No 22) leads the field with local rider David Thomas aboard, 1926.

horse and won a lot of races which helped me along. Cardiff was a good course and it is a pity that most of these small meetings have now gone.'

Evan Williams, whose father, Fred, was the starter there, set an unusual record at Ely Racecourse on Easter Monday 1933. He rode the winner, Mr Ghandi, as an amateur and the last, Vive L'Amour, as a professional jockey. A horse called Grasshopper, ridden by Lester Piggott's father, Keith, won the Club Juvenile Handicap Hurdle – the last race ever to be run at Cardiff on 27 April 1939. Thereafter, no longer would racegoers flock to Ely to witness the riding skills of the famed Anthony and Rees brothers, Bruce Hobbs, Jack Fawcus and other leading jockeys.

Douglas Leslie, whose father Colonel David Leslie was the official handicapper at Ely Racecourse for a number of years recalled: *'My father and I always stayed with Mr C.C. Williams at Llanrumney Hall, St Mellons. Squire Williams had what was known by us as 'The Hut' which was, really speaking, a wooden shed fitted out to accommodate friends for a superb picnic lunch with all the refreshment that anyone could ever ask for.*

Here one met the Hon. Mrs Violet Mundy who was one of the nicest people imaginable. Her colours were of a large harlequin pattern, and she had a useful horse called Taradidle. One unforgettable character was David Harrison who trained at Tenby. A big-shouldered fellow with a gruff voice, he trained for many of the South Wales owners and rode himself in his earlier days. His horses were ridden by the

From left to right: Evan Williams; Fred Williams, the official starter (Evan's father); Mrs Aubrey Hastings; Tommy Wilton-Pye, the Clerk of the Course.

Cardiff Races official programme.

brothers Jack and Ivor Anthony and F.B. Rees. He also had a lad called Duggan who rode his not-so-good uns, and some pretty hairy rides the poor chap used to get, too.

All the jump trainers were to be found in Squire Williams's hut, Max Barthropp, Arthur Stubbs, Miles Thompson and Bay Powell to name a few. Then, of course, there was R.H. 'Bobby' Williams, Claude Williams, old Captain Hastings Clay and Johnny Clay the famous cricketer. Mr and Mrs Harbor Homfray from the Glamorgan Hunt and their daughter, Anne, now Lady Boothby. I can also remember Ben Warner the well-known punter of those days, Tommy Andrews who won the Powderhall professional sprint, Ted Arnold the England and Worcestershire cricketer and Jimmy Wilde the world-famous boxer. Folk from every conceivable walk of life were welcome in 'The Hut' and a couple of days' racing at Cardiff were glorious fun with

Harry Llewellyn being led in after winning on China Sea at Cardiff Races, November 1937.

never a dull moment.'

Former Irish jockey H.J. Delmege, of County Tipperary, claims that it was at Ely that crash helmets were worn for the first time: *'I rode Navan Boy at the October 1923 meeting and we had to wear helmets. They were neat and weighed only a few ounces nothing like the piss pots worn now which remind me of the knights of old jousting.'*

George Holland, of Grangetown, Cardiff: *'Cardiff race days at Ely meant more pocket money. After racing a gang of us boys would descend on the track and collect all the empty beer bottles and take them back for the deposit money which was more than welcome in those days'.*

Cardiff bookmaker, Bill White, recalled visiting the track as a young boy with his father:

'As we walked to the entrance of the track the poor inmates of the hospital would be leaning over the wall begging for coppers. One of these unfortunates we got to know quite well, little Freddie we called him, my father would throw him up a couple of shillings to catch.'

Arthur Byrd, of Llanrumney, Cardiff: *'From the age of twelve, and after when I left school, I worked on the racecourse for a number of years in the weighing room where I helped to dispense drinks to the owners, trainers and jockeys who always had a stiff drink before going out to face the hazards of their profession.*

The paddock and weighing room were unique in racing as they were situated, not on the stands side, but on the cheap enclo-

Great Western Railway poster for Cardiff Races, 1890.

sure and the owners and trainers had to walk from the stands side to view the horses in the parade ring.

I saw all the well-known jockeys and owners of the time: the Anthony and Rees brothers, Willie Stott and the then amateur rider Harry Llewellyn. Then there was Lord Glanely and the leading Newport bookmaker Jimmy Jones who owned Black Isle, Lady Gay and Stow Hill. He also owned a greyhound which beat the legendary Mick the Miller in a match at Cardiff's Sloper Road Greyhound Stadium.'

Mr A.E. Pursey, of Wenvoe, who also worked at Ely as a young boy: 'After we had finished building the fences the Clerk of the Course, Mr Tommy Wilton-Pye, who was a very nice man, used to take the lads for a drink in the White Lion. Unfortunately though, I was only sixteen so I had to wait outside.'

Bob Sparkes, of Sully, can remember standing on Ely Bridge on his way home from Sunday school and watching the horses arriving by train: 'It was a most colourful sight to see the horses being led out to the carriages and walked to the race-course stables at the back of Mill Road. The atmosphere was electric just like a carnival or fun fair.'

Former rider William Hearnden: 'To me it was a lovely course, a left-handed one with an uphill gradient on the far side under the Ely Woods with well-built fences. There was a nice run-in to the winning post and the track was popular with most owners, trainers and jockeys. It was a sad loss to racing when it closed.'

The last words on the racecourse belong to Douglas Leslie: 'It was a great pity that Ely Racecourse had to disappear, for after all, it was not only a race meeting, but a great country gathering where one met all one's friends.'

Cinemas, Music Hall and Theatres

The Gaumont Cinema in Queen Street was closed in 1960 and later demolished to make way for the C. & A. Stores. Originally opened in 1887 as Levino's Hall, two years later it was renamed the Empire Theatre. A special feature of the old Empire was that it had a sliding roof which could be opened during the interval to give theatre-goers some fresh air.

Empire Theatre, 1935.

Although I recall seeing one or two stage shows there – the opera *La Boheme* was one – it was as a cinema that most Cardiffians will remember it best. I can still recall during the war years walking up what seemed to be a countless number of concrete steps to the wooden benches of the 'gods' with my mother, aunt Sarah, cousin Thelma and sister Valerie.

Later, as a young schoolboy, I used to go with my pals to the Saturday morning matinee where we would sing a song that went something like this: '*We come along on Saturday morning greeting every-body with a smile. We come along on Saturday morning knowing it's well worth-while. And members of the Gaumont Club we all intend to be.*'

Another cinema in Queen Street then was the Queens, which was the first cinema in Cardiff to show talkies. This was in 1928 and the film was *The Jazz Singer* which starred Al Jolson. During the 1950s, the Queens was renowned for showing all the horror films like *Dracula* and *Frankenstein*. And not the Hammer colour ones either! Sadly, the last film to be shown there was *The African Queen* in 1955.

Two other popular picture palaces in Queen Street were the Olympia, which opened in 1899 as Andrews Hall and is now the Cannon Cinema, and the Capitol. Opened in 1921, the Capitol provided its patrons with not only a cinema but also a restaurant, dance hall and music from an orchestra. Many famous people visited the Capitol in person and these included film star Danny Kaye, the king of rock 'n' roll, Bill Haley and his Comets, and actor Ronald Reagan who, many years later in 1981, was to become President of the USA. At 92 Queen Street was the Picture Show. On 16 December 1910 the following films were showing there: *The Wooden Leg*, *How She Won Him*, and *The Slave of Carthage* with Herr Rauscher's Austrian/Hungarian Orchestra in attendance.

The Picture Palace at 53-55 Queen Street was opened on 17 February 1911 by Sir Herbert Cory Bart, JP and the first films were: *A Lover in Europe*, *A Winning Coat* and *Why He Told Her*.

Cardiff's first music hall was probably the Coliseum which stood in Bute Street where it was said: 'Melodrama and farce (plus a pint of beer) could be had for sixpence'. Recalling the Coliseum, one old timer, long gone to that great theatre in the sky, complained of the crude exhibitions that were staged there: *'In one, a man, got up as a monkey, used to climb the scenery, resembling trees, and perform antics which would not be tolerated today. It was here that poses-plastiques were first shown in Cardiff, and the figure of a stout lady personifying Venus, perched on a large sea shell was in keeping with the style of entertainment. The price of admission was threepence, and on paying the visitor was given a small brass check which entitled him to a glass of beer at the bar.'*

Cardiff's first purpose-built theatre was the Theatre Royal opened in 1826 on part of the ground where the Park Hotel now stands. Other theatres were the wooden Circus Theatre (1876) in Westgate Street, the 'new' Theatre Royal (1878) in St Mary Street, which was later renamed the Playhouse, and the Prince of Wales Theatre.

There were other places of entertainment and these included the Grand Theatre (1887) in Westgate Street, later to be known as the Kings Theatre and then the Hippodrome Palace, and the Philharmonic Music Hall in St Mary Street.

A Cardiffian, during the Second World War, recalled the old Empire Music Hall. *'Who, of the elderly residents of Cardiff will ever forget the old Empire Music Hall? It was the most popular entertainment house in the country. What comradeship it inspired amongst the big audiences! What enthusiasm! All the 'stars' came to the Empire: Sir Harry Lauder, George Robey, Charles Coburn, Dan Leno, Marie Lloyd, Little Tich, Vesta Tilley, Harry Tate, Albert Chevalier, Zena Dare and many others.'*

The New Theatre

1996 saw the 90th anniversary of the New Theatre. Built in 1906 by the London architects Messrs Runtz and Ford, who were also responsible for London's Adelphi and Gaiety theatres, the 'New' has served its patrons well over the years. Mr Beerbohm Tree and his company performed Shakespeare's *Twelfth Night* on 10 December 1906 – the opening performance – and ever since then the 'New' has provided entertainment to suit all kinds of people.

Music Hall, Variety, opera, drama and, of course, pantomime. You name it the 'New' has staged it! Hollywood stars Marlene Dietrich, Bette Davis and Peter Lorre have trodden its boards. Other famous names who have appeared there include Anna Pavlova, Max Miller, Tommy Handley, Vera Lynn, Gracie Fields, Shirley Bassey, Tom Jones, Laurel and Hardy, Billy Cotton, Lucan & McShane – stars of the Old Mother Riley films, and Donald Peers, Wales's star of the late 1940s who was billed as 'Radio's Cavalier of Song'.

In the late 1940s my mother and father would take me to see shows like *Hollywood's Doubles* and Peter Collins's

New Theatre, c. 1910.

71

This double wooden door, pictured in 1995, was the entrance to the waxworks.

Would You Believe It? The latter show featured Belgian's Gernand Bachelard who at 9 foot 4 inches was billed as 'the tallest man in the world'.

I remember one occasion – I can't recall the name of the show – when all the acts took place in a huge glass tank filled with water. In one of the acts two frogmen dived into the tank and placed a mock limpet mine on what was supposed to be the side of a German ship. Noele Gordon (later of *Crossroads*) was given brilliant reviews when she starred in *Call Me Madam* in 1953. Our own Shirley Bassey was described as 'fantastic' when she paid a return visit by public demand in 1957. While another Cardiff performer who went on to great

things in America was 'Two Ton' Tessie O'Shea who topped the bill back in 1944.

Big-hearted Arthur Askey and Monsewer Eddie Gray delighted audiences in 1947 and way back in 1939 Hughie Green, then the 'popular young radio, stage and screen star', brought to the 'New' his 'Stars of Tomorrow' show the forerunner of his famed *Opportunity Knocks* television programme.

In 1957 a performance of Dylan Thomas's world-famous radio play *Under Milk Wood* was given. Taking the lead as narrator was Donald Houston.

The Cardiff Continental Waxworks

The famous and the infamous – Charlie Chaplin, Clark Gable, Lloyd George, Lawrence of Arabia, Hitler, Mussolini, Dr Crippen and even King Kong – all resided, or at least their wax models did, at 90 St Mary Street, Cardiff, half a century ago.

D'arc's waxworks exhibition first came to Cardiff in 1866 and stayed for three months. Later, it was to find a more permanent home at the Victoria Rooms in St Mary Street. George Lambert D'arc, who had worked at world-famous Madame Tussaud's waxworks in London, gave up his share in the Cardiff waxworks to his brother, William, when he went to China to study Chinese effigies, and to do a model of the Empress Dowager of China.

William D'arc was an uncle of Mrs Esme Barron who recalled: '*Uncle*

William and Edith D'arc outside their house in Cathedral Road, c. 1930.

William made all his own figures and the behind-the-scenes room was always littered with various pieces of wax anatomy. My aunt Edith did the dressing of the figures'.

'I remember well the policeman who looked down the stairs, the magnificent tableau of the Last Supper and the large stuffed polar bear which hugged you if you put a penny in the slot. There was also a genuine French guillotine and one of the finest replicas of the crown jewels.'

For Richard Brain: 'The Chamber of Horrors with its half light and imagined smell of hate and murder, its cut-up bits of a corpse in the barrel and a man in the electric chair gave one the creeps.' On a lighter note an object of amusement with the ladies was Catawayo the Zulu King. 'We girls used to feel under his grass skirt to find out what he was wearing under it' recalled one.

Mrs Myra Fogarty: 'As a child in the 1930s, I was taken there and I clearly remember the attendant who pretended to be a wax model. He frightened everyone when he suddenly moved!' Another lady recalled: 'In the centre was a huge gorilla [the King Kong exhibit] and he had a young girl in his arms and when you put a penny in the slot the gorilla's eyes would roll and the girl's breasts would heave'.

Anne Teeary remembers that: 'There was a large glass case with a nurse that powdered a baby when money was put in a slot'. She also recalled that the death of Nelson exhibit was 'very vivid, probably all that blood'. The waxworks must have been the only place in Cardiff in those days that opened seven days a week (10 a.m. to 10 p.m.), and Eileen Summerfield, who used to be a cashier there, recollected: 'I worked there before the war and we had lots of fun. Saturday nights were very busy especially when the

73

big rugby matches were played at the Arms Park'. The exhibits she remembered best were those of Charles Dickens, Oliver Cromwell, Tom Thumb, Tom Walls, Madame Butterfly, Hitler and Mussolini.

In 1891, on his first visit to Wales, Buffalo Bill was touring with his world-famous Wild West Show and took time off to visit D'arc's famed waxworks exhibition. Many years later, in 1975, Neath-born Hollywood film star Ray Milland on a visit to his homeland remembered being taken to *'a little museum in St Mary Street when I was a boy'*. Wax models of film stars like Anna May Wong, Clark Gable, Cary Grant and Maurice Chevalier were exhibited there in the 1930s and '40s. How sad there wasn't one of Ray Milland.

My own memories are of my sister, Valerie, taking me there nearly every Sunday after we had heard mass. I could not have been more than eight or nine at the time and the Jekyll & Hyde illusion has made a lasting impression on me. A penny would be dropped into a slot and the image of Dr Jekyll's face (the model stood in front of a mirror) would change to that of Mr Hyde's. As well as being frightened I was completely fascinated.

On 24 March 1946 the entire show was sold off and ended up at Coney Beach, Porthcawl. Earlier, some of the exhibits had gone to Billy Butlin and no doubt ended up at one of his holiday camps. Mrs Esme Barron took her grandchildren to London's Madam Tussauds in 1987 where she saw 'some familiar pieces'. She believes that some of the other exhibits were sold to someone in France. Perhaps the Joan of Arc exhibit was one of them!

Sadly, all that remains of Cardiff's Continental Waxworks Exhibition and Amusements Ltd now is the cash box that can still be seen (at least it was still there the last time I looked) half way up the steep stairs of 90 St Mary Street.

CHAPTER 3

Customs, characters and martyrs

Cardiff characters: Little Tommy Rosser

A well-known character in Cardiff during the 1860s was little Tommy Rosser who used to sell sand – which in those days was placed on the floors of most of the tiny terraced dwellings – door to door from his donkey cart. Tommy, who had a weakness for beer, never stopped for a pint on his rounds without fetching another for his beloved donkey. He was always seen in a battered top hat which he wore with the side part to the front. Tommy was forever having jokes played on him; on one occasion he called at a foundry to beg a linchpin for his cart and when he was lured into a distant part of the works his cart was hoisted to the roof of the building by rope and tackle. (Sam Allen's *Reminiscences* doesn't record whether Tommy's donkey was attached to the cart at the time!) As poor Tommy didn't have the best eyesight it was quite some time, we are told, before he managed to retrieve it.

Billy Gale

A celebrated Cardiff walker in the 1870s and 1880s was Billy Gale. A wiry little man, he performed wonderful feats of endurance walking. Billy's backers would wager that he would walk so many miles in a certain time and they invariably won their bets. They would meet in the Old Shoulder of Mutton (later the Criterion) in Church Street and arrange exhibitions of Billy's walking prowess. His first big walking exhibition took place at the Canton Cattle Market in 1876 where he walked 1,000 miles in 1,000 hours or to be more precise in just over 41 days. The following year, at the age of 45, Billy walked 1,500 miles smashing all previous records. However, in 1881, he failed in an attempt to walk 2,500 miles in 1,000 hours but he clocked up more than 2,405 miles before giving up.

Following in Billy's footsteps a quarter of a century later was Cantonian William Read who was not only a renowned walker but also a poet to boot! He is said to have broken W.H.

Broad's record for the London to Brighton race by 10 minutes at the age of 52. Like Billy he put on public displays of his powers of speed and endurance.

Mr Cough Candy

Cardiff had more than its fair share of eccentrics around this time and none more so than a street vendor who sold candy which he guaranteed would cure any ailment of the chest. He was known as 'Cough Candy' and to add to his fame he once entered a lion's den in a menagerie at Penarth Road. He never recovered from the ordeal and sadly, a short time afterwards, was said to have committed suicide in very dramatic circumstances.

Mick, Sammy, Peg, Bob

and Oh My Money

Other characters included 'Hairy Mick', a lamplighter whose face was covered in hair; 'Dancing Sammy', of Rumney, who was noted for sneering at young boys when he passed them in the street; 'Peg the Wash', an old washerwoman who used to run after children with a big stick; 'Bob Hairy Bob', who had whiskers down to his waist and who also chased the children and an old gentleman known as 'Oh My Money'. This poor soul, believed to have been defrauded of all his money, would wander the streets moaning to himself as he went along – 'Oh My Money'.

Mr Glyn Davies, of Whitchurch, who could remember when the *South Wales Echo* cost just a half-penny, recalled further characters: *'I remember Bert Jarvis who wore a battered top hat and carried a sandwich board. His hands were always well manicured and he was never without a large packet of Players cigarettes. Rumour had it that John Cory the ship owner occasionally gave him a pound. Then there was a woman nicknamed 'Penylan Sal' hopelessly drunk every Saturday night at the junction of Albany Road/City Road. Two policemen would usually lift her on to a small open truck and wheel her to the police station in Crwys Road. Then there was old Parry with a horse-drawn truck which had a boiler on the back emitting sparks as it made chips. He would shout "Chips all hot for a penny" and he lived in a whitewashed cottage in fields towards Penylan Hill '.*

Mr Davies also recalled the sad story of the woman known as 'The Lady in Black' who went every morning to the Great Western railway station to meet her husband. She would sit on one of the platform seats all day. The husband, however, had been killed in the First World War.

Lord Tredegar

Not many famous people have a statue of themselves erected during their own lifetime. One person who did was Godfrey Charles Morgan, 1st Viscount Lord Tredegar, whose equestrian statue stands in front of Cardiff's City Hall. Born at Ruperra Castle in Glamorgan on 28 April 1830, he was the second surviving son of Sir Charles Morgan Robinson the Baron of Tredegar

Lord Tredegar mounted on his charger Sir Briggs.

whose wife, Rosamund, was the only daughter of General Godfrey Basil Mundy. After being educated at Eton, Lord Tredegar, or the Hon. Godfrey Morgan as he then was, joined the 17th Lancers – 'The Death or Glory Boys' – as a lieutenant. When the Crimean War broke out he held the rank of captain and was in charge of a section of the Light Brigade that took part in the historic charge which inspired Lord Tennyson's famous poem. He served throughout this war taking part in the battles of Alma, Inkerman and Balaclava.

Sir Briggs

Before the war, Lord Tredegar's horse, Sir Briggs, on which he is seen mounted, had carried him to success in his famed purple and orange racing colours in the principal steeplechase at Cowbridge races. When Sir Briggs died he was buried in the grounds of Tredegar House near Newport and there one can see the memorial stone 'In Memory of Sir Briggs' to this day. Underneath the heading it reads: 'A favourite charger, he carried his master, Godfrey Morgan, Captain 17th Lancers boldly and well at the battle of The Alma. In the first line in the Light Cavalry Charge of Balaclava and at the Battle of Inkerman in 1854. He died at Tredegar Park, in February 1874 aged 28 years'. The statue of Lord Tredegar and Sir Briggs was erected in 1909 some four years before Lord Tredegar died.

Town crier poster, 1871.

Cardiff's Town Criers

The office of town crier is not mentioned in Cardiff records earlier than 1772. However, it is almost certain that the post dates back to ancient times. We know for certain that under a charter of 1608 the bailiffs had the power to appoint a town crier. The following men were recorded as the official town criers of Cardiff: Christopher Phillips (1772-), John Hussey (1820-), John Hussey (1836-), Edward David (1841-), John Ballard (1845-), William Llewellyn (1858-), Edward David (1860-), Morgan John (1869-), William Cox (1880-), Joseph Mountstephen (1882-), Thomas Thomas (1890-), Robert Oliver (1896-).

Thomas Thomas, who lived at Albany Road, Cardiff, was also town crier in 1891, 1892, 1894, 1895 and in 1896 he was promoted to mace-bearer. Mr Robert Oliver, of 29 Adelaide Street, who was first appointed to the post in 1896, also held the position between 1898 and 1906. William Harvey, of 18 Romily Crescent, Cardiff,

was town crier in 1907 and 1908 for which he received £10 per annum. Thomas Thomas appears to have been back in his old post in 1909 only this time the abbreviation 'hon.' appears after his name. The next name that turns up is that of Tom Rosser, who lived at 159 Keppoch Street. Mr Rosser, appointed to the post in 1909, was still in office in 1922 so he must go down as one of the longest serving town criers of Cardiff even if the post was an honorary one by this time.

As for the last person to hold the title of town crier, that honour apparently goes to Mr Thomas Kenefick of 91 Constellation Street, Cardiff. Mr Kenefick received £2 a week plus a uniform and boot allowance of £1 per annum. In the early days town criers were paid 4d or 6d an assignment. Mr Kenefick was appointed on 26 June 1922 and appears to have held the post until 1937 when the town crier also acted as a part-time messenger. The street directory for 1937 reveals that Mr Kenefick was an engine driver.

The Burning of Rawlins White

In 1555, during the reign of that zealous Catholic monarch Mary Tudor, Cardiff fisherman Rawlins White was burned at the stake for adopting the Protestant creed. An illiterate man, he was said to have become 'Very Obnoxious to the Bishop of Llandaff, on account of his religious principles'. White, who had taught himself scripture with the help of his young son who could read, had begun to 'instruct' others and at the instigation of the bishop was

Hill Street with the former South Wales Electricity Board building in the background, c. 1950.

taken into custody as a heretic. After being jailed for twelve months in Cardiff Castle, he was removed to Chepstow where threats and promises failed to make him recant. Returned to Cardiff, he was put into Cock's Tower (Cockmarel) under the Town Hall in High Street which was described as *a very dark, loathsome and most vile prison*. The time spent in his dank cell, believed to be around three weeks, before his execution is said to have been passed in *great cheerfulness and extreme fortitude*. Knowing his time had come, he commanded his wife to send him his wedding garments – a long shirt, an old russet coat and a pair of leather buskins [high boots] – which he wore on his day of execution. Then, seeing his wife and children at the place of his execution, tears trickled down his face. On being led to the stake, he fell down on his knees and kissed the ground. Arising he said these words: *Earth unto Earth and dust unto dust thou art my Mother and unto thee shall I return*. When the smith

cast a chain about him he threw up his hands and with a loud voice gave thanks to God. He told the smith: *'I pray you good friend, knock the chain fast, for it may be that the flesh might strive mightily.'* Rawlins White even helped his executioner to place straw around him and when it was set alight 'bathed' his hands over the flames.

'Whereas before he was wont to go stooping, having a sad countenance … now he stretched up himself not only bolt upright, but also a bare withal a most pleasant and comfortable countenance … that he seemed angelical'. [Foxe's Actes and Monuments of Christes Martyrs (1576 edition)

The exact spot in Cardiff where Rawlins White was executed is not known. Tradition gives two sites as the place of burning, one in St John's Square and the other in High Street. While yet another reference I have come across gives it as being in Frederick Street.

Hills Terrace, c. 1950; Frederick Street was to the right of the picture and Rawlins White was perhaps executed near here.

Hills Terrace with Frederick Street to the left of the picture, c. 1950.

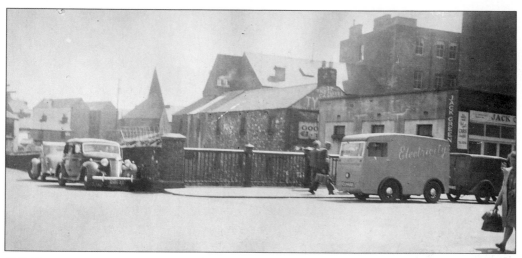

Hills Terrace, c. 1950.

The Gallows Field

The area of land near the junction between Crwys Road, City Road and Albany Road was at one time known as The Gallows Field. And as the name implies it was a dreaded place of executions.

On the Crwys Road side of the wall of the National Westminster Bank can be seen a plaque which reads: 'On this site on the 22nd July, 1679, Father Phillip Evans and Father John Lloyd were executed for exercising their priestly duties. Declared Saints and Martyrs by Pope Paul VI on the 25th October, 1970'.

At their trial in Cardiff, in the reign of Charles II, no attempt was made to convict them of treason; they were charged simply with being priests. The old *Cardiff Records* tell us that they were first dragged on hurdles to the gallows. Then they were hanged for a few moments and before they were dead they were cut down. Then, while still alive, they were disembowelled and finally dismembered. One of the main witnesses against Father Evans was a deformed man, Mayne Trott, who had been the court dwarf to the kings of Spain and England. A professed Catholic himself and married to a relative of the Jesuit priest David Lewis, who was also hanged, drawn and quartered on his 'evidence' the same year, he suddenly dropped dead shortly afterwards in a London street.

Local customs:

Roping in the Wedding

When I was a young lad, more than fifty years ago now, it was a wedding custom in Cardiff that when the happy couple returned from the church they would stand at the bride's front bedroom window and throw handfuls of coppers to the children gathered outside. A lot of pushing and shoving would take place in the street below and more often than not I came away empty-handed.

A much earlier wedding custom in

81

Junction of City Road and Crwys Road. Near here Father Phillip Evans and Father John Lloyd were executed.

Cardiff was known as 'roping in the wedding' or 'the quintaire'. A stout rope was procured and when the wedding party was on the way back from the church they were stopped by the rope being lightly drawn across the road. After the 'ropers' had been paid the wedding party was allowed to pass.

Sometimes a 'jumping block' was put in the porch over which the bride was required to scramble even though her dress could be torn in the process. In those days the groom was required to wear a leather belt as a symbol that his bride had 'something to cling to' in the future.

Funerals

On a more sombre note, I recall that before a funeral the dead person would be laid out in their coffin in the front room, so that neighbours, friends and relatives could pay their last respects. Also the curtains of neighbouring houses would be drawn until after the funeral.

Of an earlier time, Kyrle Fletcher writes: *'The Welsh people have always been famed for their funerals, and the old people of Cardiff and district were as fond of a funeral as any of their neighbours. The custom of attending funerals arose from the fact that so many of the old people were related more or less distantly to each other, and if not related either by blood or marriage, then they would be friends who knew each other intimately.*

In the smaller circles of life in the old days there was more time for the courtesies of marriages and funerals. Of course, the great funerals were those of the old – the patriarchs of the neighbourhood. They had a quaint custom of draping the room in which the dead person lay with white curtains; the bed would be hung with white, and sweet smelling herbs from the garden placed on the counterpane; while wax candles, the best that could be bought, shone all night with a mellow light in the chamber of death.

On the morning of the funeral, the mourners arrived either singly or in groups, some on foot and others on horseback. Each would be ushered into the presence of the chief mourner, who sat smothered in crape and with hanging head to receive the full honours of consolation.

In the parlour special rows of lustre mugs full of hot-spice wine were solemnly handed round, and huge slices of funeral cake were solemnly devoured. Warmed with the wine, conversation would become more general, but still with a subdued murmur, as befitted the occasion.

Usually a short service was held in the house, before which the undertaker had, with grave circumspection, handed round black gloves to the mourners: silk or kid for near relatives, and cotton for more distant members of the family. Lengths of crape would be cut off a long roll, on the understanding that the nearer the relationship the longer the strip of crape. They had one excellent custom: the bearers in turn carried the coffin to the little churchyard gate, and on the way the friends sang some of the sweet old Welsh hymns which sounded strangely, yet sweetly, on the air as the procession wended its way slowly to the church.

After the burial the crowd usually visited the nearest public house, for this was a great social re-union. In those days of hard toil and slow travel, relatives had but few opportunities of meeting except at a funeral, and then all the news of the family would be exchanged'.

William and Gladys Bryant, 1930.

The Bute Dowry

In 1897 the 3rd Marquess of Bute wrote a letter to the Mayor of Cardiff which commenced:

'My dear Mr. Mayor, – The silver wedding of my wife and myself falls upon April 16th. We have always retained the most lively recollection of the kindness with which we were received, not only by the Corporation, but also by the people of Cardiff, upon our wedding day. It has occurred to me, as a memorial of this twenty-fifth anniversary, to place in the hands of the Town Council the sum of £1,000 the yearly income of which should be annually given to some girl of the poorer classes in Cardiff whose marriage might be impeded by the want of such sum'.

Surprisingly when the Bute Dowry

William and Gladys Bryant (née Taylor) of Cathays were married in 1930. Longer wedding dresses, as opposed to that worn by Gladys, only later became fashionable.

public notice was placed in the local paper there were no nominations. However, the following year, 1898, Alice Mary Green, the daughter of City Hall porter Sidney Green, and Ely Paper Mills worker, William Tanner, became the first recipients.

In those days the happy couples would be driven to the City Hall in a horse-drawn carriage. Once there, the programme of events went something like this:

1. The Town Clerk to examine the marriage certificate.
2. The Mayor to explain the origin of the Dowry.
3. The Town Clerk to read the first eleven verses of the second chapter of the Gospel.
4. The Mayor to hand over the amount of the Dowry (in gold sovereigns).

5. The Mayoress to present the Bible.

If the recipients were really lucky a local jeweller would give them a wedding ring and a baker often gave them a wedding cake.

War-time recipients in 1941 were Miss May Hewitt, of Amherst Street, a munitions factory employee and her fiancé John North who worked at Dowlais Steelworks.

The Bute Dowry is still in existence to this day with the Third Marquess of Bute's original investment of £1,000 in government stock, nearly 100 years ago on, still earning interest. One thing for sure, though, there are not so many applicants these days.

CHAPTER 4

Transport, disappearing dockland and three ships

Horse-drawn cab crossing Hayes Bridge Road, c. 1890.

Electric tramcars in Queen Street, c. 1904.

Horse-Drawn Trams

A correspondent writing to the *Cardiff and Suburban News* in 1944 had this to say: 'When I came to Cardiff in 1900 the horse-drawn trams were still in evidence. They certainly did not hurry and it was possible to commence a walk level with them at some particular point and outdistance them easily. I did this many a time. The horse-buses, however, were much faster. There was a particularly good service via Park Place to northern Cathays and back via City Road, then known as Castle Road.

I saw one of these old trams in a corner of a field in Llanishen a few years ago; it was being used for storing tools. There was a good service of horse-cabs in Westgate Street and near the railway stations. You could get a 'growler' to take you from one end of the town to another for the very moderate charge of half-a-crown, baggage included. The cabbies were characters, courteous and good humoured. A couple of hansom cabs were also obtainable. The drivers of one of these invariably wore a tall white hat and was a very original character.

A number of shoeblacks [shoeshine boys] plied their trade in the main thoroughfares. One of them had a pitch by the Monument, at the top of St Mary Street, and there were two others at the railway station approach. Bute Street, also, was a recognised area with the shoeblacks. Most of their customers were the coloured seamen who were going up town, and took special pride in well-polished boots and shoes, smart ties and button holes. Like the horse-trams the shoeblacks have disappeared over the years.

An interesting feature of the town was the Hungarian Band. The band, all genuine Hungarians, consisted of eight members, and they played daily at various points [including Ely Racecourse whenever meetings were held there] throughout the spring and summer. Two of their frequent pitches were Queen Street and the junction of Newport Road and Clifton Street.

They wore dark-blue uniforms and boarded together at a house in Riverside, and it was quite a pleasant experience to hear the strains of the Blue Danube waltz and La Thiere's Silver Birds as one walked down Queen Street or along Newport Road'.

Electric Tramways

The *Evening Express*, dated 1 May 1902, informed its readers that: 'At noon today the Cardiff Corporation Electric Tramways were successfully opened for traffic, amidst the general rejoicing of everyone concerned, and Cardiff can now claim to be one of the progressive towns of the kingdom which have adopted electricity for traction purposes'.

Earlier that day, twelve tramcars, dec-orated with imitation flowers and flags bearing the Welsh dragon left the Clare Road depot for the town hall where the Mayor, council officials and invited guests were waiting to be taken on a trip around the town. Some £380,000 had already been spent upon the new tramways and when completed the total cost would be around £$\frac{1}{2}$ million pounds. The first route opened was between Castle Road, renamed City Road three years later, and the docks.

Purpose-built depots at Newport Road and Clare Road housed the trams which had been built by Dick Kerr of Sheffield. The trams which were 'comfortably fitted and brilliantly illuminated' were open-top double-deckers. So successful were these electric trams, which had replaced two private companies operating horse-drawn vehicles, that two years later there were 131 of

One of the early trams in Queen Street, c. 1902.

Electric tram outside Central Market in St Mary Street, c. 1903.

them transporting 18 million passengers a year on 12 different services round the town. Single-deck and double-deck trams transported Cardiffians to their places of work and pleasure. Owing to so many of the staff being on active service during the First World War, services were curtailed and it was decided to employ women as conductresses for the first time.

Demise of the Tram

A prototype double-deck covered-top tram took to the streets in 1923 and this was so popular with the public that a further 80 were bought, with the last of them arriving in 1925. However, in 1931 motor buses replaced trams on the Cathays route and by 1939 the Corporation had decided to replace trams with trolley buses. On 20 February 1950 the last Cardiff tram made its final journey on the Whitchurch Road route. It was lit by hundreds of fairy lights and a notice on its side read: *'To all of you old-timers – and you still in your teens. Who drove with me through peace and war – packed in just like sardines. I'd like to thank you one and all for the patience you have shown, and say farewell to the Finest Folk that a tram has ever known'.*

During the First World War women were employed as conductresses.

The last Cardiff tram, 1950.

Cardiff Castle lock on the Glamorgan Canal.

Old Glamorganshire Canal

Many Cardiffians deplored the filling in of the old Glamorganshire Canal in the 1950s. Excavated between 1790 and 1798, the Glamorganshire Canal, which was opened in 1794 as a means of transporting iron from Cyfarthfa, near Merthyr, to Cardiff Docks, was one of the picturesque features of old Cardiff.

Twenty-five miles long with some 52 locks, the canal flourished for more than a century. The £103,600 cost of its construction was met by traders and Merthyr's ironmasters.

By 1890 the business was running at a loss, however. Part of the main canal was closed down in 1900, but it was not until 1942 that the last barge passed down it.

From North Road the canal followed the path of the old town wall and moat. On the east side of Cardiff Castle it travelled under Kingsway through what is now a pedestrian subway. From there it passed along The Friary to what was appropriately called The Tunnel. Some 115 yards in length, this took the canal under Crockherbtown (Queen Street) and then continued south through what is now St David's shopping centre. From there it followed the course of the old town ditch which lay beneath the buildings on the eastern side of Working Street. Passing under Hayes Bridge Road, at the Hayes Bridge–Caroline Street junction, it flowed south-westerly by Mill Lane, where the Holiday Inn now stands, and passing the Custom House it continued to Cardiff Docks.

One old Cardiffian reminisced: 'On the return journey along the route to Merthyr the barges were loaded with grain and flour which was stored in the canal company's warehouse, of which my father was manager, for local delivery. The night shift from the works would have a booze up which would lead to arguments and a fight in the street. The fighters stripped to the waist, used bare fists and sometimes the fighters ended up in the canal'.

Mrs Joan Anthony recalled: 'We, as children, loved the old, patient barge-horses coming along with the loaded barges. When the horse was coming along, you had to pin yourself to the old stone wall, almost. You'd see the huge hoof come down, and maybe a loud snort from the horse almost putting you off-balance! It was a rural scene down North Road in those days, boys leaning over fishing and at Kingsway people

The North entrance to the Castle, North Road.

would throw pennies into the canal and the boys would dive for them'.

Sadly, all that remains now of the Glamorganshire Canal in the Cardiff area is some 1,500 yards at the Forest Farm Nature Reserve in Whitchurch.

HMS Havannah

An old 42-gun frigate called HMS Havannah, which had been one of the ships that had accompanied Napoleon to St Helena in 1815, sailed into the Cardiff East Bute Dock in 1860. The intention was to fit her up as a training ship, but the Admiralty declined to supply the rigging and other equipment and the idea was abandoned.

Later transferred to a more permanent berth on the side of Penarth Road, near Penarth Bridge, the ship was converted to an industrial school known as the Cardiff Ragged School. 143 feet long and 36 feet wide, the Havannah, which had been built in 1811 at a cost of £18,259, became the home for 80 or so destitute and homeless children who slept in hammocks and wore uniforms of

91

HMS *Havannah*, c. 1880.

white round caps, blue blouses and white trousers. On leaving the school many of the children were found employment in domestic service, shops, warehouses, foundries and collieries while others joined the Army or Navy.

The Medical Officer of Health declared in 1888 that the old ship had become a 'decaying hulk' and that 'age and weather has rendered her topsides too rotten to be made watertight by caulking'. Then in 1905, the *Havannah* was sold to Mr Henry Norris, of Cowbridge Road, for £1,030 and broken up. Mr Norris kindly presented Cardiff Corporation with two of her cannons which were placed in Roath Park. During the First World War, however, the cannons were melted down as scrap metal. The ship's bell, meanwhile, went to the Vicar of St Sampson's church in

Grangetown where the *Havannah* pupils had sung in the choir.

HMS Thisbe

The frigate HMS *Thisbe*, which took four years to build at Pembroke Dock, was launched in 1824. Some 151 feet in length and 40 feet in breadth she had a tonnage of 1,083 tons. Rated fifth in the naval service, she was in commission for 19 years and was stationed in Devonport. At the request of the Marquess of Bute, the *Thisbe* was loaned by the Admiralty for the purpose of a mission church to seamen on 13 August 1863.

Positioned first in the East Bute Dock, her gun deck was fitted out as an institute and church for the seafaring community. In the reading room below deck, seamen could read all the local and national newspapers and they were also provided with stationery. There was a resident chaplain aboard and regular church services were held as well as magic lantern shows and concerts.

When the more permanent Seamen's Church and Institute in the West Dock was built in 1892, the *Thisbe* was sold to Mr W.H. Caple for £1,000 and he had her broken up near the old Cardiff low water pier. Sometime afterwards the town clerk of Cardiff, Mr J.L. Wheatley, presented to Cardiff Corporation the figurehead of the *Thisbe*, which had been preserved by him, and it was placed in Roath Park.

HMS Hamadryad

The Illustrated Guide To Cardiff (published by the *Western Mail*, 1897)

HMS *Thisbe*, c. 1865.

informs its readers that the *Hamadryad* was 'an old 21-gun frigate'. But in Dr John Mayberry's *I saw Three Ships* it is described as 'a 46-gun frigate'. However, one thing we can take for certain is that the *Hamadryad* was towed from Plymouth and berthed in the Cardiff East Dock for the purpose of a seaman's hospital and was opened on 1 November 1866.

Said to have been built in Pembroke Dock at a cost of nearly £25,000, this old ship, which had never seen active service, was later moved to a more permanent site on waste land near the old Glamorgan Canal sea lock.

At a cost of nearly £2,800 the ship was fitted out for her new role ready to receive around 60 patients. There was accommodation for a doctor, his staff, the matron and several nurses. Voluntary contributions of two shillings per ton of cargo carried by registered ships visiting the dock helped to finance the running of the hospital.

Right up until the Royal Hamadryad Hospital was built in Ferry Road in 1905, the HMS *Hamadryad* performed a great service to sailors, many carrying infectious diseases. Some years later she was towed to Appledore and broken up. The ship's bell which was rung at both six bells and eight bells throughout her career, along with the figurehead, can

HMS *Hamadryad*, c. 1870.

Bute Road, better known as Bute Street, c. 1950.

be seen in the Welsh Maritime and Industrial Museum in Cardiff Bay.

The Bute Road

Kyrle Fletcher (*Cardiff Notes: Picturesque and Biographical*) gives us an excellent description of the Bute Road of old:

'From the Canal Bridge on the Hayes a long straight road leads down to the Docks. Tramcars run swiftly up and down the Bute Road, but the adventurer may prefer to walk down the most cosmopolitan thoroughfare in any city in Europe. The Tower of Babel has gone ages ago, but the varied languages of Babel can be heard any day on the Bute Road.

Next to the shop signs, written in almost every language under the sun, the strangest features of the Bute Road are the smells. As you walk the pavement you pass a long train of coolies in slippers, wearing curious round caps, all walking in procession one behind another. A cluster of swarthy Greeks smoking cigarettes at a doorway, stand to stare at a group of midget Mongolians wrapped in rough sheep and goat skins. That tall man in navy blue serge might have been a Viking from Norway, with his fair hair and massive frame, instead of a mate from a Scandinavian ship. The Greek boarding-house sends out a whiff of Turkish tobacco and rank garlic.

The Chinese are standing in crowds round their laundries or tobacco shops. Most of them wear some portions of their native dress, either Chinese shoes or quaint caps, but the Japanese, a few doors lower down the street, all wear European dress.

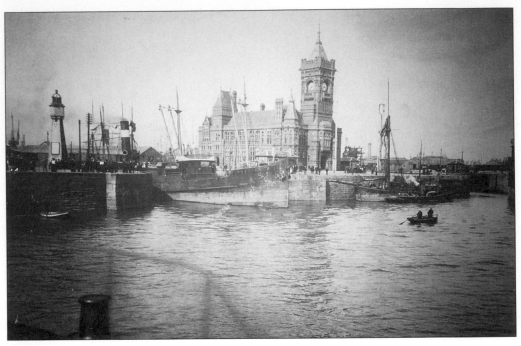

Docks scene, c. 1900.

These two Eastern races are curiously alike, yet unalike, for while the Chinese look out across the road with lack-lustre eyes, as well befitting the descendants of an ancient race who can claim to have been civilised when our forefathers were but savages, the Japs are all keenness and animation, chattering together as though life was a very good joke, even though they are stranded so far from their Eastern Islands.

The Italians are fairly numerous, noisy and light-hearted, usually singing and laughing together and smoking those rank cigars which even a veteran smoker will be wise to avoid. There are Arabs and Armenians in gay dress, giving a touch of the gorgeous East to the otherwise drab surroundings. The negroes have their settlement in the side streets behind the Bute Road, but they come out and parade in all the glory of white spats, velveteen suits and light hats, adding their Christy Minstrel effect to the general motley assembly.

The Danes and Swedes, with broad-built Dutchmen, seem to keep very much to themselves, and are seldom met with in the street fights in which the visitors from more Southern climes occasionally indulge. In the season, groups of onion boys from Brittany, with their picturesque wide-brimmed hats, parade with strings of onions, leaving a strong odour in their train. The Greek Priest, the Scandinavian Missionary, and the Jewish rabbi are also to be seen, each walking in the solitary seclusion of his office.

Of course there is a police station on the Bute Road, and a parish church, resembling an Eastern building, and replacing the famous old parish church which once stood at the end of St Mary Street. All down the one side of the road the railway runs on to an embankment, above which rise the high walls of a famous sea-biscuit factory, and one can imagine how the sailor, home from a long voyage, turns from the sign of ship's

Another early docks scene, c. 1900. The sign on the lamp-post reads: 'Beware of the Engines'.

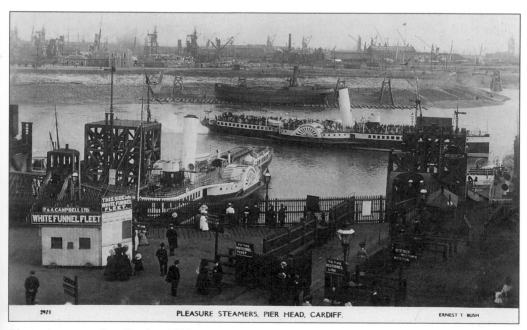

PLEASURE STEAMERS, PIER HEAD, CARDIFF.

Pleasure steamers, Pier Head, c. 1925.

The offices of Crawshay of Cyfarthfa, West Wharf, c. 1897. The gentleman in the picture is apparently Mr Watkins Lewis the manager.

biscuit to seek a loaf of new bread in the baker's shop on the corner. Down the other side are the various boarding-houses with shops below, from which, as you pass, comes the mingled odour of garlic, opium, fried fish, oil skins, Turkish cigarette and tar ropes, the very smells of Babel. This long road is the connecting link between Cardiff and Cardiff Docks, and the various nationalities are proofs of the trade which *links Cardiff to so many distant places'.* This then was the Bute Road of Kyrle Fletcher's days.

West Wharf, c. 1897.

Tiger Bay

There have been many versions of how Cardiff's Tiger Bay got its name. But the explanation I like best was published by the South Wales and Monmouthshire Record Society nearly half a century ago in the book: *The Place Names of Cardiff*.

It reads: '*In 1871 and later there was a first-class society headed by Mr Harry Moreton, and at one of their entertainments a new singer became very popular. He had a song of a descriptive kind called Tiger Bay and nightly brought Bute Town into it. Soon after this Bute Town was called Tiger Bay*'.

The song was almost certainly sung at the Coliseum in Bute Street. Cardiffian Peter Godwin said it was sung to the tune of *Goodbyee*, a First World War song, and that it went something like this: '*Tiger Bayee, Tiger Bayee it's not very far from the docks. Once you get to Loudoun Square take the first turning there, Tiger Bayee, Tiger Bayee*'.

A disappearing dockland, c. 1967. The Pier Hotel is seen towards the right of the picture.

East side of South William Street, c. 1967.

Torbay Hotel, Margaret Street, c. 1967.

The Packet Hotel, Bute Street, c. 1967.

Stan Cottle's betting shop, Dudley Place, c. 1967.

The Convict Ship

Cardiffian Stanley Adams, who worked as a telegraph boy, recalled going aboard the notorious *Martinière* when she was berthed in the Queen's Dock in the 1930s. This was the ship which took convicts to Devil's Island off French Guiana, once a year. The rest of the time she worked as a coal carrier. Mr Adams remembered that '*the dock postman allowed me to take the mail aboard with the instructions to hand it over to the chief steward. Unfortunately, I was unable to get down to the hold where the convicts were imprisoned and any mutiny by them was ruthlessly suppressed by scalding from the permanently fitted steam pipes*'.

The Days of Sail Long Gone

A correspondent writing to the *Cardiff & Suburban News* in 1927 had this to say: '*The days of the old windjammers – otherwise sailing ships – seem to have left us for ever. Often as a boy I have stood on Cardiff Pier Head and witnessed the sailing of long ships. The old shanties sung by the sailors and the farewell tears and cheers of women folk used to make up a scene which must linger in the memories of those who loved the real sailorman.*'

Pleasure Steamers

Many Cardiffians will have happy memories of paddle steamer trips to Weston-super-Mare and Ilfracombe. Pleasure steamers have operated in the Bristol Channel for more than a century. The *South Wales Daily News*, dated 25 August 1887, carried several advertisements for excursions and one of these adverts announced that there would be a 'Marine excursion from Cardiff to Ilfracombe by the New Clyde-built Royal Mail saloon steamer

Stuart Street.

Waverley, the greyhound of the Bristol Channel (weather and circumstances permitting)'. The return fares were five shillings or three and sixpence and there was a band and refreshments aboard. Another advertisement in the same paper read: 'Daily service between Weston and Cardiff by the saloon steamer *Lady Margaret* (wind, weather and circumstances permitting)'.

Mutiny in Cardiff

In 1887 a ship sailing from Cardiff was involved in a mutiny and a murder. On 11 May Captain Piren of the Glasgow barque *Willowbank* sailed into Falmouth and reported that on 25 March he had spoken to the *Occidental* which was en route from Cardiff to Acapulco. The *Willowbank* had met the *Occidental* when she was 68 days out of Cardiff and the chief mate of the steamer had signified his wish to speak to Captain Piren. He was told that when the *Occidental* had been 30 days out signs of dissatisfaction were noticed among one or two of the crew. The captain had dealt with the malcontents firmly and it seemed that the mutinous sentiment had been quelled. However, on the 56th day out an Irishman named Moriarty sought an altercation with the captain. He insulted the skipper and in a scuffle he drew a knife and plunged it into the captain's chest. Moriarty was secured with difficulty and it was found afterwards that the Irishman has been encouraged in his murderous intentions by a section of the crew.

Louisa Street, c. 1967. Ken Jones's betting shop is partly obscured by a coal delivery lorry.

Dudley Street, c. 1967.

Cardiff Castle Hotel, George Street, c. 1967.

The large building on right is the Atlas Preservative Company Ltd, George Street, c. 1967.

West side of George Street from James Street, c. 1967.

Penarth Terrace, c. 1967.

CHAPTER 5
Miscellany

Colonel William Frederick Cody, better known as Buffalo Bill.

Billy Brian riding on one wheel, Roath Park, c. 1905.

Trick Cyclist Supreme

Billy Brian, who lived in Whitchurch, was arguably Wales's greatest-ever trick cyclist. A silver cup now in the possession of his son, also known as Billy, reads on one side: 'For cycling backwards from Newport to the Moon and Stars, Cardiff, without dismounting' and on the other side: 'The Lee Cup presented to W. Brian, 4th April 1904'. The great German trick cyclist Bud Snyder, who was appearing at the Empire Theatre, begged Billy to join him in his act but he was turned down with Billy content to stay on with Spillers and Bakers where he worked as a clerk for forty years. Billy junior also recalls that his father did all kinds of balancing acts on his bike, that he cycled backwards around Roath Park Lake and up Leckwith Hill and Thorn Hill and won numerous other trophies in the process. He was still doing his trick-cycling routine when well into his 50s and in later years he devoted himself to learning to play the piano so that he could continue entertaining people.

Billy Brian performing one of his balancing acts, Roath Park, c. 1905.

When Buffalo Bill Came To Cardiff

Buffalo Bill, American scout, expert horseman and buffalo hunter, Pony Express rider, showman and legendary folk hero visited Cardiff in 1891 with his famous Wild West Show.

Colonel William Frederick Cody, to give him his real name, also brought with him the legendary sharpshooter Annie Oakley and a seven-year-old Red Indian boy believed to be the only survivor of the Battle of Wounded Knee. The boy had been found on the battlefield by Chief No Neck.

Some 200 Red Indians, Mexicans and cowboys along with 200 horses and 18 buffaloes arrived in three trains of 25 carriages and, on the banks of the River Taff in Sophia Gardens, set up their camp and villages of tepees, cowboy tents and stables. Twenty thousand people attended the opening performance when 42 Wells lights, said to be of 18,000 candle power each, were used to light the arena.

One of the highlights of the show was Buffalo Bill's re-enactment of single-handed combat with Yellow Hand while the Pony Express display, in which a chain of ponies was stationed around the arena, with the rider literally springing from one saddle to another at amazing speed, also had the audience entranced.

Some spectators doubted whether the natives were bonafide. Fred Cadd, who lived in Station Terrace, Cardiff, who had been connected with the Poplar River Agency for 14 years before returning to Wales, was able to tell them that they were 'undoubtedly genuine'. He

Official programme for Buffalo Bill's Wild West Show.

had actually traded with Sitting Bull for buffalo robes and when he asked the Indians about Sitting Bull they told him he was 'tka' (dead), adding that he had been a fool.

An advertisement in the *Western Mail* described the show as 'The Most Colossal Amusement Enterprise that ever visited Wales' and the Great Western, Rhymney Valley and Taff Vale railways ran special trains from the Valleys, Carmarthen, Chepstow and Cheltenham for the thousands of visitors who paid either a shilling for the cheapest seats or four shillings for the dearest.

'Buffalo Bill is Coming' announced

An advertisement which appeared in the *South Wales Graphic*.

CARDIFF SOPHIA GARDENS FIELD.

ONE WEEK ONLY,
Commencing Monday Afternoon, July 6th.

BUFFALO **BILL'S**
WILD **WEST**

And Congress of Rough Riders of the World

The World's Greatest Educational Exhibition,

HERO HORSEMEN OF ALL NATIONS

The Orient & Occident

Now Touring the Provinces

Col. W. F. CODY,
("Buffalo Bill,")

another advert in the paper for D'arc's famed Waxworks Exhibition in St Mary Street.

Little wonder that Buffalo Bill's next visit to Wales in 1903 was looked forward to with great anticipation. A record crowd of 22,000 people packed Sophia Gardens and sometimes more than one hundred horses were in the arena at the same time, the display including Red Indians from the Sioux, Arraphoe, Brule and Cheyenne tribes in full war paint. *'Right through Wales, from Bangor and Rhyl in the north, and through the south, I have been more than delighted with the reception which has been accorded to the show and to myself. If for no other reason I am naturally pleased with the excellent financial results,'* said Buffalo

Bill.

The following year – 1904 – Buffalo Bill made his farewell visit to Wales bringing with him 800 men and 500 horses. A number of interesting additions had been made to the programme. One of these was Carter the Cowboy Cyclist. This act had the audience holding their breath. Carter used to ride down an inclined platform of 92 feet, at a speed said to be 60 miles an hour, and jump across a chasm of around 42 feet landing on another incline. The mock battle of Custer's Last Stand and the Raid on the Deadwood Stage Coach, meanwhile, remained great favourites with Cardiff audiences.

In his honour, the Mayor of Cardiff invited Buffalo Bill to a dinner at the Mansion House, During the evening he told the guests: *'The scenery in Wales would be hard to excel. The mountains, hills and streams remind me of my own native land. It is grand, it is beautiful and we are leaving with a great deal of regret'*.

Buffalo Bill, however, would fall from 'riches to rags'. The man, who in one season alone killed 5,000 buffaloes to provide fresh meat for Irish navies working on the railroad, died penniless 13 years later in 1917.

Cardiff Fine Art, Industrial and Maritime Exhibition

Cardiff had never before, or perhaps since, staged anything like the Fine Art, Industrial and Maritime Exhibition of 1896. It attracted a million visitors from all over the country. The Taff Vale Railway Company brought thousands of people down from the valleys and dropped them off at a purpose-built station on the exhibition site – where the City Hall, Law Courts and Welsh National Museum now stands. As well as the industrial and mining exhibits, there were plenty of side-shows to amuse and entertain. These included an 'African' jungle with live lions, tigers, crocodiles and alligators.

A local paper reported that *'Cathays Park in a comparatively brief space of time underwent a wonderful transformation, as if some magician had laid on it his all-powerful hand. But it had taken scores of builders, carpenters, plumbers, gas fitters, smiths, painters and so forth several months to bring about the great change'*.

In the evenings the exhibition area was lit by 10,000 fairy lights and running the whole length of the site was an artificial lead-lined canal (containing 200 tons of lead) which was illuminated by thousands of prismatic gas lamps. There were coracles, water cycles and boats for hire on the specially-built lake.

The Grand Concert Hall was the scene of banquets, balls and band concerts, and on one evening 10,000 people watched a concert by a 500-strong choir. Some 20,000 people turned up for a military tournament while the open-air Santiago Opera attracted thousands to every performance. There were weekly track and field contests as well as amateur and professional cycling. Other attractions included Borland's Electric Railway, the only one of its kind at that

The entrance to the Cardiff Fine Art, Industrial and Maritime Exhibition of 1896.

The lead-lined canal at the Cardiff Fine Art, Industrial and Maritime Exhibition.

time entirely controlled and lighted electrically; the Switchback Railway, which was 1,000 feet long; an exact replica of Shakespeare's House; and an Old Cardiff replica. The main entrance was a decorated horseshoe archway, 40 feet in height, and the portal was flanked by two towers crowned with Oriental domes.

HM Queen Victoria gave her patronage to the exhibition and it was visited by the Prince of Wales (later King Edward VII) the Princess and their two daughters. It was on this occasion that the first public performance in Cardiff of 'animated screen photography' – better known as moving screen pictures – was shown by Birt Acres.

When the exhibition closed after six months on 7 November 1896, hundreds of men waited around the gates in the hope of finding employment. From a spectator's point of view it had proved a magnificent success although financially only a small profit was made.

Borland's Electric Railway.

The 'Old Cardiff' replica.

Exact replica of Shakespeare's House.

The Maritime Section.

Empire Games, 1958

In 1958 Cardiff hosted the sixth British Empire and Commonwealth Games. And like thousands of other Cardiffians, I had the pleasure of watching the track and field events at the Cardiff Arms Park.

We thrilled to the sight of seeing the great Australian Herb Elliot win the mile in under four minutes. New Zealander Murray Halberg breaking away from the field with three laps to go to take the three miles and Australian Dave Power pipping Wales's own John Merriman in the six-mile event. Power went on to win the marathon and the atmosphere was electric when he entered the stadium after his gruelling 26-mile run.

The boxing was held at Sophia Gardens and Cardiff's Malcolm Collins (seen in the picture carrying the flag at the opening ceremony at the Arms Park) won his second boxing silver medal at these games in the feather-weight class. There were those boxing critics who thought he should have been awarded the gold medal.

Although as a runner, I was never good enough to take part in the games I did play a small part in them. I was one

Boxer Malcolm Collins carrying the Welsh flag. Author Brian Lee is seen standing to the right of him with arms folded.

This javelin thrower stood atop Howell's building in 1958.

of the escort runners to Ken Harris, a former Commonwealth Games athlete. It was the job of the escort runners to run alongside Ken from the Cardiff Royal Infirmary to the Arms Park where he handed over a silver-gilt baton that contained a message from the Queen. Ken passed the baton to former Olympic Games sprinter and Welsh rugby international Ken Jones who in turn passed it on to the Duke of Edinburgh to read out at the opening ceremony.

I also took part in the official film that was made of those wonderful games. The camera crew had me running up hill and down vale pretending to be different relay runners carrying the baton that was eventually handed to Ken Jones. I never did get to see the film and suppose I never will now.

'My father was a groundsman at Cardiff Arms Park where the athletics took place and one of his many duties during the games was to pick up all the broken winning tapes which, by the way, were made of genuine Welsh wool. He collected all the lengths and brought them home. I was thirteen then and with the wool I started to knit a pair of booties for my eldest brother's wife who was expecting a baby. Unfortunately though I only had enough wool for one bootie. Eight years later I appeared on TWW's television game show Claim to Fame and ended up beating the panel'. Mrs Burt, Heath, Cardiff.

Air-Raids

On 18 May 1943 the Germans bombed Cardiff killing 45 of its citizens. Two thirds of them died when a land mine was dropped on residential homes at St Agnes Road in the Heath.

My earliest memory is of the early days of the Second World War and my mother wrapping me up in a blanket and carrying me downstairs to the Anderson air-raid shelter at the bottom of our garden at No 23 Thesiger Street. Crouched below some two feet or more of earth, in our reinforced hideout, my mother, my sister and I would huddle together and listen for the sounds of the German air-planes. In time we could tell theirs from ours. The damp, musty smell of that air-raid shelter is something I shall never forget.

There used to be a chimney sweep in

our street who used the air-raid shelter in his garden to dump all the soot he collected as his large family usually stayed indoors during the bombings. But this particular night with it being a rather heavy bombing raid they had no alternative but to jump down the air-raid shelter for cover. And when the all clear siren sounded they emerged unscathed, but covered in soot!

I remember my uncle Philip Donovan, putting me in the carrier of his grocery round bicycle and cycling around Cardiff to survey the bomb-damaged streets. I distinctly recall him cycling over Woodville Road bridge and I only have to pass that spot today for the memory to come flooding back.

I recall my mother warning me not to pick up anything in the streets for fear it might be a butterfly bomb. Apparently the Germans used to drop very tiny bombs which looked like propelling pencils. Well, that's the story mother told me.

During one air-raid, my aunt Sarah, cousin Thelma, sister Valerie and mother and I were watching a film in our local cinema (the Coronet in Woodville Road), when the air-raid red alert was sounded. In the dark and confusion that followed my mother got outside of the cinema to find she was holding the hand of the wrong little boy!

Bombed houses in St Agnes Road, Heath, 1943.

Western Mail & Echo staff with the gas masks they collected before the start of the Second World War.

Anderson air-raid shelter in the garden of a house in Pearl Street, Splott.

Police headquarters staff at Canton, 1895.

Cardiff Police Force

The Cardiff Police Force is said to date back to 1836 when Mr Jeremiah Box Stockdale was appointed Superintendent to train and organise men recruited locally. The first police-man to be appointed was a 'pensioner' and former shoemaker called Tom Pen-y-Bont. The three others were another old man called Howells, Jeremiah Jones, a knife grinder, and a Mr Audrey who was made a sergeant.

In the early days, the Cardiff Police Force were equipped with rattles for use when they needed assistance. Constables were employed by the Glamorgan Canal Company and Taff Vale Railway while the Bute Docks Police Force was set up around 1860. An advertisement in 1836 read:

'Borough of Cardiff

Wanted two police officers, each officer to be the age of 21 years, but not to exceed 40. Salary 15 shillings a week and a set of clothes. Any person desirous of the appoint-ment is required to attend at the Guild Hall, Cardiff, having previously sent to the Mayor his name, address, age and a refer-ence of character.'

Cardiff Fire Brigade

Two manual engines were housed under the old Town Hall in High Street in 1880. But as far back as 1739 a manual fire engine had been kept in the porch of the church tower at St John the Baptist Church with the church

Chief Constables and Inspectors at Canton, 1895.

Mobile Police cars at Canton, 1945.

sexton having the responsibility of looking after it.

In 1866 a steam engine drawn by horses was acquired at a cost of £224. Brass helmets, and a new uniform, were issued for the first time in 1880 and ten years later sub-fire stations had been set up at Roath, Canton, Cathays and Grangetown. In 1883 a fire engine house was built at the rear of the new Town Hall in Guildhall Place just off St Mary Street.

A new fire station in Westgate Street was opened in 1917 and on 30 March 1973 the new Fire Services Headquarters and Central Fire Station was opened at Adam Street by the Rt.

Hon. Lord Mayor, Alderman Mrs Winifred Mathias.

Temperance Town

The area of land now known as Wood Street and where the Central Bus Station and the Great Western Station now stands was once called Temperance Town. It was originally known as The Bulwarks (on the River Taff). This derelict area was formerly a mud pit and was subject to floods during the period of high tides or when the River Taff was in flood. It was sold by

Cardiff Fire Brigade, c. 1896.

Superintendent G. Geen (centre of foreground), with Cardiff Fire Brigade, old station yard, 1913.

Colonel Wood to Mr Jacob Scott Matthews who had the area levelled for building purposes.

A strict teetotaller, he made it a condition that no alcoholic drinks were to be sold in the area. During the development of the land the great temperance orator Mr J.B. Gough held meetings in a large booth which is said to have been erected where Gough Street – named after him – was built.

An adjoining street, Eisteddfod Street, got its name because the National Eisteddfod had been held in the vicinity. Matthews also built a hall for the promotion of teetotalism. Alderman Trounce is his reminiscences claims that: *'Primarily the hall was used for the advocacy of temperance, but I have known it to be used as a circus, a dancing saloon, a concert hall, and now it is doing its best work as one of the most successful* *places of worship in Cardiff, the Wood Street Chapel'.*

Arcadia

A feature of Cardiff has always been its arcades. The oldest is the Royal Arcade which dates back to *c.* 1858. Eight shops were said to have been opened at first and a further forty added sometime later. An old resident of Cardiff recalled that when he was a little boy living in the Valleys his mother having returned from a shopping expedition in Cardiff told him of 'the splendid new street with a glass roof.'

The High Street Arcade, opened between 1880 and 1887, was designed so that one could walk from High Street directly to St John's Square. Originally

Looking from Westgate Street towards Wood Street and Temperance Town.

fifty yards long, it had 34 shops with offices above.

The Castle Arcade, which runs from High Street to Castle Street, was opened by the Mayor of Cardiff, Alderman David Jones, on 28 October 1849. To honour the occasion the arcade was bedecked from end to end with bunting and shrubs. It was built by Alderman Daniel Lewis, who had a furniture shop there, from the plans of architect Peter Price. In 1988 it underwent a £500,000 refurbishment.

Morgan Arcade, perhaps the best-preserved of Cardiff's Victorian arcades, is named after David Morgan who started out in business with a gentlemen's outfitters on The Hayes. The building of this arcade is said to have '*altered the whole aspect of this part of the city, it swept away a nest of slums, some picturesque courts or so-called gardens. At the St Mary Street end it wiped out a large house with a large garden belonging to a well-known Victorian figure in Cardiff, Mr Charles. At The Hayes it cleared away the Union Buildings, consisting of 33 houses and small shops and an inn. Thus was the old centre of Cardiff changed.*'

The Wyndham Arcade, with its glass roof supported on iron arches, was built around 1887. It has seen better days and there is talk of demolishing it. It is a rather dull and dismal arcade, but one person who had happy memories of it was Ethel Williams who, after she left there to run a stall in the market, told a local newspaper, some thirty years ago:

Royal Arcade, c. 1910.

'Tears rolled down by face when I left my shop there for the last time. I still often stroll through the arcade and think of the old days. But they weren't all good days. It was quite a rough place at times. There was a doss house at the top of the arcade in Mill Lane and we used to get a lot of meth drinkers there.'

Other arcades in the central area of Cardiff are Andrews Arcade (1896) and Dominion Arcade (1921), both in Queen Street; Duke Street Arcade (1902) which leads also into High Street and St John's Square.

Duke Street Arcade, c. 1910.

Morgan Arcade, c. 1910.

Llanrumney Hall

Llanrumney Hall, which is now a public house on a large council estate, was once known as Llanrumney Monastery. In days long gone the monks, to celebrate St Melo's feast day (October 22), used to organise an annual sports and jollification day. The main event was a foot race from the monastery to St Mellons church and the winner received a most unusual prize. His reward was the monastery's sanctus bell which had a blue clapper. However, he did not keep it for more than a few hours as his prize was really the honour of restoring the bell for use in the monastery.

In later years the race finished at a spot that is now the site of the Blue Bell Inn, St Mellons, and this is one explanation as to how the pub got its name. The Blue Bell Inn was built chiefly to provide accommodation for the gentry and their horses, who came from different parts of the parish and who attended St Mellons church.

According to a very old local newspaper, Llanrumney Hall was the burial place of Llywelyn Ein Llyw Olaf, the last Welsh Prince of Wales. The newspaper claimed that ancient manuscripts, and tradition, assert that: 'The headless body of Llywelyn was interred at

Llanrumney Hall, c. 1990.

Llanrumney Hall, the fine old Elizabethan mansion standing in its well-wooded park at St Mellons on the confines of Cardiff'.

Apparently, after Llywelyn was killed in a skirmish with some English soldiers near Builth Wells, his head was dispatched to King Edward I, who was staying at Conwy Castle. Llywelyn's headless body, however, was alleged to have been secretly brought by the monks to Llanrumney Hall which in those days was known as Little Keynsham, on account of its close association with Keynsham Abbey in Somerset.

Somewhere there is supposed to exist a statement in writing by the granddaughter of a Mr Moggridge, who once owned Llanrumney Hall, to the effect that her grandfather's workmen discovered in the vaults of the hall a stone coffin, placed in a very thick wall of masonry, which contained the remains of Llywelyn Ein Llyw Olaf, whose body had never before been found.

The historian Professor Freeman, who once resided in Llanrumney Hall, also believed that the remains found there were of the last Welsh Prince of Wales. No wonder Llanrumney Hall, the birthplace of the famous buccaneer Sir Henry Morgan, is said to be haunted by two ghosts!

Llys Tal-y-bont

Cardiff Council employees attending training courses at Llys Tal-y-bont will probably be unaware that the old building is steeped in history. Situated at the lower end of Parkfield Place just off North Road, the former farmhouse is said to date back to the thirteenth century and is believed to stand on the site of the Court and Palace of the Princes of Glamorgan.

The noted Welsh historian, Professor William Rees, claimed that Llys Tal-y-bont (the court at the head of the bridge) was 'the last link with much ancient Welsh history'.

John Hobson Matthews (*Cardiff Records*) tells us that '*On the eastern bank of the Glamorganshire canal, where the canal approaches within about a hundred yards of the Taf, stands a rambling thatched farmhouse popularly known as Lislabont or Islabont (Llystalybont). Although it looks insignificant today, this is one of the most ancient residences in Glamorgan*'.

Tenants of Llys Tal-y-bont in days gone by had to agree to do 20 days annual military service at Cardiff Castle to his lord. Llys Tal-y-bont ceased to be a farm in 1918, and in the early 1920s the buildings were used for commercial purposes.

It was also said, at one time, to have been occupied by Catherine Griffiths, a servant who was hanged for robbing her former employers on 7 October 1791. From Llys Tal-y-bont Catherine went out and stole from the houses of many Cardiffians before being caught.

Griffiths confessed that she had burgled houses as far away as London, Bath and Bristol. Found guilty and sentenced to be hanged from what was known as the 'Heath Oak', she was driven by horse and cart from Cardiff Castle to this old oak tree in nearby Heath Park. Catherine confessed her crimes on the spot and begged the sheriff to be allowed to be buried in a coffin. Her last request granted, she helped fix the rope to the tree for her own execution.

Llys Tal-y-bont farmhouse, c. 1970.

ACKNOWLEDGEMENTS

First of all, I would like to thank Margaret O'Reilly of the South Wales Echo, as without her help, as I have already mentioned in the introduction, this book may never have been published.

I would also like to thank Chalford Publishing's Project Editor Simon Eckley for having faith in this book and also for his assistance in the layout of the text and photographs.

Special thanks go to BBC Wales's Frank Hennessy for writing the foreword at a time when he was busy with his radio work and pantomime rehearsals.

I am grateful to the staff of the Cardiff Central Library Local Studies Department (especially J. Brynmor Jones) for their help.

For the loan of photographs, I am indebted to the following: Matthew Williams, Keeper of Collections at Cardiff Castle, Norman Hopkins, Neil Jones, Phil Street, Roger Bellringer, Phil Hall (who took some of the Docks photographs), Paul Crippin and George Frantzeskou, Bill Brian, Harry Welchman, Bill Surringer, Matthew Nicholls, Cardiff County Council and Western Mail & Echo Ltd.

Also to all those former readers of my 'Looking Back' column in the *Cardiff Independent* who sent me photographs and who planted the seed of an idea for this book.

My apologies go to any contributors who may have been omitted from these acknowledgements.

Finally, my thanks to my wife Jacqueline for her forbearance.